Charles Willson Peale

THEY MADE AMERICA

A series of biographies under the editorship of

CECILE HULSE MATSCHAT   ALLAN NEVINS

CARL CARMER   LEWIS PAUL TODD

Stephen F. Austin: Father of Texas BY CARLETON BEALS

Charles Willson Peale: Artist and Patriot BY BERTA N. BRIGGS

George Rogers Clark: Soldier in the West BY WALTER HAVIGHURST

Red Jacket: Last of the Seneca BY ARTHUR C. PARKER

Alexander Hamilton: Nation Builder BY NATHAN SCHACHNER

(Additional books in this series are being prepared.)

Charles Willson Peale

ARTIST & PATRIOT

BERTA N. BRIGGS

McGraw-Hill Book Company, Inc.

NEW YORK TORONTO LONDON

*In quoting from the diaries, letters, and memoirs of
Charles Willson Peale, the author preferred not to correct Peale's errors in spelling or his lapses in grammar.
Writers of the period, and George Washington was
no exception, followed their own dictates in spelling,
capitalization, and punctuation. As they stand, Peale's
writings have an endearing naïveté, and his mistakes
are no reflection upon his intelligence.*

CHARLES WILLSON PEALE: *ARTIST AND PATRIOT*

Library of Congress Catalog Card Number: 52-9763

To Cecile Hulse Matschat

Preface

THE FINE ARTS could not take their place in American life until the struggle for bare existence became less pressing and means for luxuries became available in well-established settlements. The first native paintings appeared in response to a desire on the part of the well to do to have likenesses painted of themselves and their families. Since there were no trained artists, sign painters and other craftsmen tried to meet this demand, and their naive, wooden-faced "effigies" formed the first step in the development of American painting.

The gradual unfolding of the art of portraiture in this country is exemplified in Charles Willson Peale's career. His first efforts, handicapped by lack of instruction, were stumbling. Determination to master the art and ceaseless striving to better his work led to a solid command of portraiture in his middle, highly productive years. Admirable flexibility in adapting himself to improved methods of painting resulted, in his old age, in some of his finest work.

The secret of Peale's prodigious accomplishment was his ability to concentrate on the task in hand. Personal concerns, his very joys and sorrows, took second place to his work. Like other early Americans he was a born craftsman, able to master any skill he wished to acquire. Like them, he was adaptable and ingenious, inventing tools when none were available; he was challenged by difficulties and tempted by unconquered fields.

Circumstances had deprived Peale of a formal education, but his active mind constantly reached out for information, which he gained from books, from his fellow men, and through intelligent observation. The knowledge gained gave him so much satisfaction that he longed to share it with others; thus Peale's Museum was born. Everything that he did expressed his generous, loving spirit and zest for life. His paintings are warm with the geniality that his kindliness and charm aroused in his sitters. He was a man of uncommon goodness—a fine painter and a great human being.

Americans owe Peale a debt for services which his painting rendered. He preserved the flavor of the gracious life of Maryland and Virginia in his portraits, a life which otherwise would have had no visual representation. Had he not painted portraits of men of the Revolution and leaders of the early years of the republic, most of these men important in the early days of our nation would be names without faces today.

The author is indebted to the American Philosophical Society in Philadelphia, owner of the larger part of the Peale papers, for its gracious permission to use quotations from the artist's memoirs, published in part in the two-volume biography of Charles Willson Peale by Charles Coleman Sellers. She is also appreciative of the privilege of using transcripts and photostats of Peale's war diaries in the Frick Art Reference Library in New York City.

BERTA N. BRIGGS

Contents

Reproductions of a selected group of paintings by Charles
Willson Peale are to be found following pages 134 and 150.

1

His Father
Comes to the Colonies

THE BRIGHT May sun gilded the grimy walls of London's
Newgate Prison. But there was no sunshine in the cell into
which Charles Peale had been locked by a surly guard.
The shadow of the gallows lay upon him, for he had just
been sentenced to death for embezzlement. Not many days
were left him; he would be hanged on May 24 of that year,
1735.

The slight, graceful young man seated on the hard bench
of his solitary cell did not have the appearance of a criminal. His costly clothing was worn with the easy assurance
of a gentleman. The fine-featured face and brilliant blue
eyes were alert and intelligent. Debonair Charles Peale
for the first time in his agreeable life was facing inescap-
able reality. Up to now he had lived in a fine dream world
of his own making.

Charles Peale came of a line of country parsons who
served the long, square-towered Gothic church in Edith-
weston, Rutlandshire, that dominated the stone houses
and hedge-bordered lanes of the pretty English village.

1

As eldest son, following an established family custom, he was destined for the church. Therefore he was given an unusually good education at the grammar school at Oakham, the county seat. There he liked to walk past the Norman castle, counting the horseshoes on its rugged stone walls. By ancient tradition, these horseshoes had been given by kings, queens, and peers who passed through the town. Judging by their number, there must have been much royal traffic through the years. From the grammar school Charles went to St. John's College, Cambridge, to prepare for the ministry.

Before he left home for Cambridge, he learned that he had been named heir to a rich uncle, Dr. Charles Wilson, with the understanding that the estate must provide an income for his surviving daughter during her lifetime. The glittering prospect of future wealth gave the young student delusions of grandeur, which did not promote serious application to his studies. Instead he led a gay and extravagant life, convinced, as the months went by, that the church was no career for him.

The college authorities apparently agreed with him on that point. At any rate, Charles left abruptly for London. He went in all confidence that he could find means of making a living until he inherited his fortune, for he had many assets. He was uncommonly handsome with a charming, ingratiating manner. He had a sound classical education, was good at figures, and had exceptional skill in penmanship. This equipment, backed by the influence of family friends, secured him a clerkship in the London General Post Office.

At first he copied documents and examined accounts. He

performed these duties so well that he was advanced to more responsible tasks. He now opened letters containing money, kept account of them, and sent out receipts signed by the proper officials. Since his penmanship was artistry of the highest order, Charles found he could imitate the signatures of his superiors on papers acknowledging monies accepted and thus appropriate a remittance now and again with no one the wiser. The post office was notoriously corrupt, and the young clerk was doubtless following the example of men higher up who had methods of lining their own purses. Since such dishonesty was fairly common, his offense possibly did not seem wrong to Peale. It was delightfully simple and made life pleasant for a young gentleman who loved fine clothes and good living. But success bred carelessness, and inquiries on the part of a woman client brought Peale's embezzlement to light. He had appropriated the staggering total of nineteen hundred pounds! Charles had indeed lived well in London. Arrest followed, then trial, and now Charles Peale was awaiting execution.

Before the fatal twenty-fourth came around, Charles was notified that his sentence had been commuted to banishment to the American colonies. His life may have been saved by a committee in London that was organized to rescue from prison skilled craftsmen and well-educated men who would make useful colonists. By whatever means the reprieve had come about, Charles felt that exile was a vast improvement over annihilation, and he left Newgate thankful that snowy lace, not a harsh rope, was his neck gear.

He left no debts in London; the post office remittances had kept him solvent. Either because of a blind spot in his conscience or because he felt that his crime had been expiated by imprisonment and exile, he seemed to feel no responsibility to repay the money he had embezzled. At any rate, for the present he had no choice but to set sail for America.

Peale secured passage on a wretched little sailing vessel bound for Virginia and, full of optimism, embarked on the long, dreary voyage. Surely the new land would offer opportunity to a bright young man. After endless weeks at sea the green shores of Virginia were a welcome sight to the handful of passengers, weary of maggoty food and damp, crowded quarters. Charles stepped ashore at New Post on the Rappahannock River without a shadow of his crime upon him. The wife and family he subsequently acquired apparently never became aware of that dark chapter of his life.

With astonishing brashness Peale immediately sought a political appointment on the strength of his former position in the London post office. However, no government job was forthcoming, and the need for earning a livelihood was pressing. Teachers were in demand. What better employment for a former student at Cambridge! No one knew that his university career had been brief, and Charles proceeded to pave the way for his entry into the teaching profession.

A notice appeared in the *Virginia Gazette* announcing that Charles Peale had published "An Essay towards rendering the Rudiments of the Latin Tongue more easy and agreeable to the Capacities of Children; also to advance them in the better Understanding of their Native Tongue." No copy of the essay exists, but making learning more agreeable to children was a novel approach to education at that time. No wonder Peale became a popular and successful educator.

His ideas attracted attention in the right places, with the result that Peale became a teacher in King William's School in Annapolis, Maryland, an excellent institution, founded in 1696 by subscriptions from wealthy colonists. The school, which in 1784 received its present name, St. John's College, numbered among its graduates a large proportion of the important men of Annapolis.

Peale liked his new surroundings. He felt at home with the familiar British names of the streets—Duke of Gloucester, Prince George, Cornhill—and found the brick houses, hip-roofed with wide chimneys at their gable ends, pleasing. The school was near the State House, which stood on the highest point in the city, commanding land which sloped down to the Severn. Church Circle was not far. There was situated St. Anne's Church, a Church of England parish closely allied to King William's School. It was the custom for schoolmasters to assist in the service, and this duty also fell to Charles Peale, so lately escaped from the gallows. As he walked along the school grounds, he admired a noble tulip poplar under which, he was told, in 1632 a treaty was signed with the Indians. Could he have looked into the future, he would have seen his eldest son taking part in patriotic demonstrations under that same tree, then to be known as the Liberty Tree.

Peale entered easily into the social life of Annapolis; his polished manners made him welcome everywhere. One evening, at a small party, he met a sprightly widow of his own age, Margaret Triggs Matthews. She was an attractive, plump girl with a twinkle in her soft gray eyes. She danced a minuet with Charles, and later they joined a group singing glees and madrigals, her clear soprano making a pleasing contrast to his baritone. There was a warm motherliness in her nature, which appealed strongly to a young man beginning to long for a home of his own.

Their congeniality, established at their first encounter, led to frequent meetings. Charles and Margaret were soon on terms of close intimacy. Before long, marriage was not only desirable to both but immediately necessary to avoid the scandal which would arise when gossips ticked off the months between marriage and a baby's birth. Charles left King William's School and secured a position at a free school near Centreville in Queen Annes County, well across Chesapeake Bay and far from gossipy acquaintances. There they could happily await the arrival of their first child, who would be known and honored in history as Charles Willson Peale, portraitist of the American Revolution.

2

A Boy Grows Up
in Maryland

CHARLES WILLSON PEALE was born with a silver spoon in his mouth, according to the registration of his birth:

Charles Willson Peale, son of Charles Peale by Margaret, born April 15, 1741, which Charles as he says is the Eldest Son of the Reverend Charles Peale Rector of Edith Weston in the County of Rutland and heir . . . [to] the Estate of Charles Wilson. . . .

Mention of the legacy in the sparsely punctuated record of his baby's birth shows how large it loomed in the father's mind. For years expectation of wealth hung like a golden mirage over father and son. When money was scarce, they were sustained by hope of financial security ahead. Yet as the dream failed to materialize, it bred frustration. The mirage grew bright at times but finally, following the habit of mirages, faded forever.

Though the child was obviously named for his rich great-uncle, his name has two *l*s in the record. This spelling persisted; he was always Charles Willson Peale.

When the little boy with double *l* in his name was two

years old, his father stepped up in his profession to become headmaster of Kent County School near Chestertown, Maryland. The spacious school building provided pleasant living quarters for the Peales on the floor above the classrooms. The windows framed fine views of the Chester River, always alive with boats of all kinds—many white sails and the occasional elegant barge of a rich planter rowed by slaves in colorful livery. Everyone traveled by water in Maryland. In her ragged shore lines were inlets and tidal rivers without number, while roads were few, rough, and without bridges over the many streams.

Little Charles's home was comfortable but not luxurious. The furnishings included "six rush chairs, two armchairs, two large chests, an old couch, a pine table, a tea table, a corner cupboard, pewterware and earthenware." Not a word about beds. Perhaps the family had to share the one old couch.

The family rapidly increased. Motherly Margaret Peale had a succession of pretty, healthy, blue-eyed babies upon whom to lavish her love. Margaret Jane followed Charles; next St. George, born on that saint's day; then James; and last Elizabeth Digby. Peggy Durgan, Margaret's orphaned niece, helped with the children, and in the kitchen there was an indentured servant working out the cost of her passage from England. She looked forward to being a freewoman one day.

Charles Peale was an ardent horseman. In the stables he had "a grey bantam horse, a grey fox-hunter, a grey mare and a colt," probably gray. As soon as Charly's legs were long enough, he was taught to ride the bantam horse and showed promise of becoming as good a horseman as his father.

Charles, Sr., was respected as an educator. Kent County School was advertised in the *Maryland Gazette* as an institution "where Young Gentlemen might be boarded and taught the Greek and Latin Tongues, Writing, Arithmetic, Merchant's Accounts, Surveying, Navigation." Also included in the curriculum were fencing, dancing, and drawing.

Charly (as the younger Peale always spelled his nickname) attended classes in Latin and mathematics and did well in his studies. But he liked the drawing lessons best. He had a natural gift for handling crayons and the sharpened sticks of graphite called pencils. He copied engravings of European paintings accurately and even attempted an original sketch of Adam and Eve, inspired by a reading of Milton's "Paradise Lost." When he first entered the drawing class, he admired the work of a much older boy, John Beale Bordley. Charly shared his father's affection for this extremely shy youth, and he saw that the schoolmaster's kindness and sympathy were helping his friend to be more at ease with people. John had such a genuine thirst for knowledge that Charles Peale could not resist giving him additional lessons outside school hours. This generosity was to yield dividends for Peale's family in later years when Bordley, a successful lawyer, was established on his prosperous plantation on the Gunpowder River near Annapolis.

Charly was growing rapidly. He was slenderly built but strong and agile. His father wrote a friend, "He is just such another dirty, wading sloven as I remember myself at his age." Evidently he was a perfectly normal boy. His fine blue eyes were keenly observant, and his hands were clever at any task. He saw with concern that his parents were increasingly troubled about money matters. Charly knew that tuition fees were not paid promptly and that Charles and Margaret found the necessity for taking boarding pupils irksome. The boarders made so much extra work for Charly's mother, busy with her lively family, that he wished he were old enough to help his parents. He wanted to do something more than carry instruments for his father when he did surveying for nearby landowners to increase his insufficient income.

Charles Peale wrote to England from time to time to inquire if his cousin were still alive. Unfortunately for him, she seemed gifted with longevity. He needed that legacy. Overwork, worry, and increasingly severe attacks of gout weakened his constitution. He had no resistance to overcome an undiagnosed ailment which caused his death at the age of forty-one. He died disappointed because he had never attained the prominence which wealth could have brought him. Yet he was widely mourned as a man of fine character and respectable achievement.

With his death the family income ceased, and the rooms above the school had to be vacated at once to make room for the new master. Margaret Peale sold the gray horses and shipped the household goods to Annapolis by barge. She soon followed with the five children, Peggy Durgan, and the indentured servant. Her plight was desperate; there were no Peale relatives in America to turn to, and she herself had no kin to help her. John Beale Bordley, out of appreciation for the helpfulness of his former schoolmaster, came to the rescue of Charles Peale's family. Out of his ample means he provided Margaret with enough to maintain a modest home and feed the children.

The Peales settled into a small brick house that was crowded but made cosy and homelike by Margaret. Despite her sorrow, she kept a cheerful atmosphere for her children. She was a woman of too much spirit and pride to accept help for long. As soon as possible, she sought work to provide a living for her family. Happily, Margaret was skilled in fine needlework, trained from infancy, as were most colonial girls, to wield a needle competently. There was an excellent market in Annapolis for embroidery and dressmaking; Maryland women were noted for their fashionable attire.

No drab homespuns for the ladies of the great plantations! They rustled about in satins, brocades, and laces imported from England along with news of the latest London styles. British ships tied up at the wharves of Annapolis to unload cargoes of furniture, fabrics, clothing, china and porcelain, tea, and spices. They returned laden with the wealth of Maryland, tobacco, which the English wanted for their own use and for profitable sale on the Continent. The captains of these vessels frequently acted as shoppers for the tobacco growers. It was usual for them to sail for England entrusted with lists of luxuries to be purchased in London with proceeds from the sale of "sotweed," as tobacco was vulgarly known.

Annapolis, one of the most important cities of the colonies, was unsurpassed in luxurious living and magnificence of dress. No city in England of comparable size could rival it. In the autumn the rich planters and their families flocked to Annapolis for a season of social gayety, which came to a climax with the horse racing in November. Races were the favorite amusement of the Marylanders who imported fine horses from England and bred them for racing. When the races were over for the day, dinners, balls, and theatrical performances in one of the oldest theaters in the colonies filled the evenings.

Charly Peale spent hours watching the stream of richly decorated sedan chairs carried by slaves in livery and smart carriages drawn by shining horses which transported their exquisitely dressed passengers through streets bordered with trees brilliant in autumn foliage. He had a sharp eye for the details of feminine attire, which he would sketch out roughly when he got home to keep his mother abreast of the latest styles. For himself he stored up memories of soft tints—lovely blues, mauves, and gray-greens. He cared little for strong colors. As Charly stood watching the brilliant passing show, he may have seen, though unaware of his name, a tall young Virginian, George Washington, who came to Annapolis whenever he could to follow the races and to enjoy the plays.

As a result of such emphasis on fashion, Margaret Peale was kept busy with as much work as she could turn out. Anyone in the household who could sew a seam was pressed into service. Charly contributed more than fashion notes. He drew patterns for embroidery which embellished the garments his mother made and suggested harmonious color combinations. He had time for this because Margaret could not afford to send him to one of the better schools. What schooling he obtained had to be from a free school, which taught only writing and elementary "reckoning."

No matter how fatiguing the day had been, Margaret Peale devoted an hour in the evening to singing with the children and her household. The little Peales were naturally musical and were able to sing in parts with accuracy and sweetness of tone. Their pleasure in making music formed a bond that held the family together over the years.

When Charly had passed his twelfth birthday, he was eligible for training in a craft; he was old enough to be apprenticed to a master craftsman. Margaret hesitated to apprentice a gentleman's son, but this appeared to be the only way of equipping him with training for a useful career. He would be lodged, fed, and clothed by his master for seven years, and she would be relieved of his support. She was a levelheaded, practical woman who refused to gamble on vague hopes of an inheritance.

She and Charly talked over various crafts and decided at last that saddlery offered a good future; there would always be a market for saddles and harnesses. They chose as master saddler "Nathan Waters, Saddler, at the house of Mr Wallace, opposite to Mr James McCubbin's Store on Church Street."

Church Street, which ran from Church Circle to the wharves, was in the area set aside for trades and shops. Annapolis was strictly zoned. Desirable land along the water front was occupied by the fine mansions of the wealthy. The common people had their own quarter, while tanneries and breweries were banished to the edge of town most remote from the dwellings of the aristocrats. Their superior nostrils must be spared noxious odors.

Nothing now remained for Margaret Peale but to sign the agreement with Nathan Waters and to see Charly safely under his protection. With her son's hand in hers, she walked briskly toward Church Street.

3

An Apprentice
Learns About Love

THE DOCUMENT which made Charles an apprentice has not
been preserved, but it must have read like this:

This Indenture witnesseth that Charles Willson Peale, Son of
Margaret Peale of Annapolis, aged thirteen years or there-
abouts, with the consent of his Parent and also of his own Full
and Voluntary Will hath put himselfe Apprentice unto Nathan
Waters, Saddler, of ye same town, and ye said Trade which
Nathan Waters now useth, him to be taught and with him after
ye manner of an Apprentice to Dwell and Live from ye day
hereof until ye full end and term of seven years.

Charles pledged himself to serve his master well, not to
waste his goods nor to gamble. He was not to marry while
an apprentice. For his part Waters promised to furnish the
boy with "Apparell, Meate and Drinke and Bedding and
all other Necessaries meete and convenient." At the end of
the term he was to "Supply his Apprentice with two goode
and sufficient Suits from head to foot."

The mutual promises contained in the indenture protected both master and apprentice. The arrangement was

almost universally successful, and probably no more recent system has been more effective in training good craftsmen. The bond could be revoked and the boy returned to his family if he showed no aptitude for the chosen trade. Charles was determined not to let that happen to him.

It was hard for Margaret Peale to leave her cheerful, helpful boy under a stranger's roof for seven years. She would miss him at home. However, it was comforting to know that he was on the way to a useful career.

Once under Waters's roof Charles had no time to be homesick. First of all he donned the strange new working clothes with breeches fronted with leather. They were cut extremely full so that, when he was engaged in a sedentary task, they could be worn front to back, bringing the leather to where the wear and tear came. The boy did not like the fearful stink of the roughly tanned hides, which were brought to the saddlery from tanneries at the far side of town. The hides had to be soaked for many weeks and then scraped to a suitable thickness with long, sharp knives. Next, oil was pounded into the leather to make it supple. It was hard, dirty labor and the hours were endlessly long, but Charles worked at it with a will until he had learned to prepare a skin properly. It was all very different from drawing designs for embroidery. The reward for conquering this phase of the craft was initiation into the next steps in constructing a saddle. He learned to carve the base, or tree, from beechwood and then to cover the wood with layers of cloth and glue to keep it from warping. Next, padding was added, which had to be carefully placed so that it would chafe neither the horse's back nor the rider's bottom. The final process was the delicate matter of cutting the leather to pattern and fitting it with glassy smoothness over the basic structure.

Charles was a serious worker who found real satisfaction in mastering the various steps in the work. He was eager to excel in every technique taught to him. His attitude was an agreeable surprise to the master. Waters was used to apprentices who needed the stimulus of a beating to keep them at work, boys who, after an exhausting day's work, still had energy left to get into mischief. He was committed by bond to be responsible for their behavior and to make them good citizens, but he also had another interest in training them well; skilled apprentices were his best possible advertisement as a craftsman. Peale was especially in his favor because he saw in the boy the makings of an expert workman. He was amused to see how vainly the other boys tried to draw Charles into their pranks. "Sobersides," they jeered at him. Charles was quite content to be a sobersides; he had little taste for mischief.

After several years of Charles's term had passed, Waters felt that Peale's exceptional devotion to his work and his growing skill entitled him to exceptional privileges. He asked the lad if he would care to take on repair jobs outside the shop. He could have the fees he earned.

Charles was nearly speechless at the dazzling prospect of earning some money for himself. He managed to find words to thank Waters for this chance and awaited his first commission with impatience.

Peale hoarded his earnings until he had enough money to buy a watch. With a fat watch ticking in his pocket, he felt like a man of substance. Alas, it did not tick long, for it was a most inferior watch. The Annapolis watchmaker charged five precious shillings to repair it. Soon it stopped again. This time Charles determined to repair it himself. He took it apart briskly. But when it came to putting the works back into the case, the wheels and springs seemed to have multiplied and showed a devilish reluctance to settle into place.

Peale was furious. He would learn how to mend watches. He would get the better of this business! The local watchmaker amiably answered his questions and revealed a few tricks of the trade. Patiently, the lad experimented with his own timepiece until he knew what made it tick. He had mastered a new skill and little knew how useful it would be to him in the future.

It took longer to save up for the next purchase. Many of the plantations where there was repair work to be done were beyond walking distance. A horse was a necessity if he were to reach them. He was seventeen by the time he had saved enough to buy a serviceable horse. That purchase made him feel he was really getting on in the world.

Having a horse to ride gave Charles a chance to enlarge his social life. Now he could visit acquaintances he had made at the saddlery or at Waters's home. After church on Sunday he was free to do as he pleased, and it pleased him to go calling.

There were no blue laws in Maryland like those which made Sunday a day of gloom in New England. The Church of England prevailed in the colony, though all faiths, including the Roman Catholic, were welcomed to Maryland. The original charter granted to Lord Baltimore promised tolerance for all forms of religion. Once the Marylander had done his duty by going to church on Sunday morning, he could spend the day pleasurably with a clear conscience.

One fine Sunday afternoon Peale set out to visit an agreeable youth by the name of Brewer whom he had met several times under Waters's roof. Before mounting his horse, he drew on spatterdashes, loose cotton pantaloons which protected a rider's breeches from dust, mud, or water spots. Brewer lived at West River, a deep inlet of Chesapeake Bay, bordered by a stand of great oaks which provided timber for the shipyards.

Charles was not sure of his way. The so-called roads were little more than old Indian trails except for occasional "rolled roads," which had been smoothed by hogsheads of tobacco constantly rolled from curing sheds to private docks along the water front. Whenever Peale saw a house, which was not often for they were widely scattered over the countryside, he stopped to ask directions. The great plantation houses looked like hens surrounded by chicks, for they sat in the midst of a group of smaller buildings— smokehouses, milk houses, cabins for slaves, chicken runs, and stables. He always looked for martin houses, miniature replicas of the mansions set on poles near the big house. The families of martins which inhabited these apartments set up a fearful din if they saw a hawk approaching, thus warning the householders to look to the safety of their poultry.

In the clearings the great fields of tobacco looked like soft green velvet. Along the trails Charles amused himself by counting the kinds of birds he could name. Cardinals flashed through the green leaves like sudden flames, and their soft whistle delighted his ears. Doves cooed in the thickets, and a woodpecker hammered industriously on a hollow tree. Once, fording one of the innumerable streams, Charles started a great blue heron which flapped off noisily on its great, wide wings. Later he disturbed an egret in all the beauty of its mating plumage as it solemnly fished in a stream.

Suddenly a big, comfortable-looking house appeared in view. Peale thought that it must be the Brewer home. Seeing no one outside, he tied his horse to a post, removed the spatterdashes, and tidied his light-brown hair. When he looked into his pocket mirror, he saw a long, thin nose, a firm, well-rounded chin, mobile lips, and deep blue eyes. He was interested only in seeing if his face was free from mud spatters.

Assured that his appearance was neat—he was always careful about that—he walked up to the house door and knocked firmly. From within came a fresh young voice, "Go 'round to the back, you impudent baggage."

An odd greeting, Charles thought, but he walked obediently to the kitchen door, which stood wide open, emitting a mouth-watering odor of roasting meat. At the enormous fireplace two pretty girls were watching a small "spitdog" running in a hollow cylinder which set in motion the spit on which the joint was browning. They were startled by Peale's arrival and greatly embarrassed. Fourteen-year-old Rachel blushed deeply, for it was she who had called out so rudely to someone she thought was a forward slave knocking at the door.

At the sound of a strange voice Mrs. Brewer came running into the kitchen. To Charles, she was a gorgeous vision in a red and gray gown patterned in large trees, a canary-yellow satin apron, and an elaborate lace cap festooned with ribbons. She was all apologies for her child's rudeness and tried to make up for it by lavishing hospitality on the visitor. Young Brewer joined the party, and to the relief of hungry Charles, they sat down to an abundant dinner. At the eighteenth-century plantation houses, provision was always made for unexpected guests, whether friends or strangers. Inns were few and so inferior that travelers avoided them whenever possible.

After that Sunday, Charles rode out to West River as often as he dared, for he had promptly fallen in love with lively, brown-haired Rachel. Conviction grew with each succeeding visit that she was the girl he wanted for his wife. He soon began to feel that she looked upon him favorably. The fact that three years remained of his apprenticeship, during which he had promised not to marry, did not deter him. Solemnly he asked Mrs. Brewer for permission to pay court to her daughter. Fourteen years seemed a little young, even in those days of early marriages, but Rachel's mother gave her consent. Charles might woo her child.

The businesslike youth lost no time. Completely unsophisticated in such matters and fully confident that Rachel would accept him, he burst in upon her where she sat in the garden with an older sister. Without the slightest preamble he blurted out his proposal, "Will you marry me?" Just like that! Rachel was dumfounded; her tongue failed her.

Charles repeated his question more emphatically. Rachel was still speechless.

Hurt and disappointed, he took her silence for refusal. Rudely he shouted that he would give her one hour to make up her mind. Whipping out his treasured watch, he glared at it glumly.

That made Rachel furiously angry. At the end of the
hour she refused to reply. Charles recorded the episode in
his memoirs, which were always written in the third person:

The Lady's resentment prevented any reply. The time expired. He went immediately into the House and thanked her
mother for the kind entertainment he had received, and said
he hoped Miss Rachel would get a better husband than he could
make. That he must now take leave of the family forever, but
the next Sunday he called at Mrs. Brewer's to get his whip
which in the hurry of leave-taking he had forgot. He then made
only obedience to the family and afterward rode to West River
to see a Lady with whom he had some acquaintance in several
visits to his Master's family. And finding the Lady at home, he
asked to speak in private with her and began to declare his intentions of seeking a Lady that might make him a wife. He
asked her If she had any engagements on her hands? The Lady
was confused and seemed at a loss to answer such a question
but she faintly intimated that she had. He replied that he was
sorry for it but that he would give her no further trouble and
very politely took his leave of her.

Charles felt he had wasted altogether too much time in
trying to get a wife. He decided to apply himself to his work
with extra diligence and forget about unappreciative females.

Weeks later, quite by chance, he encountered Rachel
Brewer at the gate of her aunt's house in Annapolis. Charles
spoke to her, saying that he regretted the circumstances
which kept him from visiting her at her home. Rachel replied tartly that the circumstances were all his fault. If he
thought she could be bullied into marrying anybody, he
was wrong. What a way to try to win a girl's heart! Her

brown eyes were snapping, her cheeks glowed red with anger, and she tossed her curls disdainfully.

Charles begged her to excuse his clumsiness. He had been in love and eager for her consent. Could she forgive him? Could he come to see her again? Rachel, mollified, agreed to let him come out to the plantation on Sunday. "Mamma will be glad to see you."

On that Sunday, in the garden, Charles quietly and tenderly asked Rachel to be his wife. This time she said "Yes."

They were engaged, but marriage was out of the question until the term of apprenticeship ended. For two years the devoted swain rode out to West River every Sunday regardless of the weather. The horse needed no guidance; he knew every step of the way.

Unexpectedly Waters made Peale a proposition. He offered to shorten the term of apprenticeship by four months if Charles would take over the entire responsibility of the saddlery while he went to Bermuda. Charles jumped at the chance. He carried the whole weight of the business with happy enthusiasm, working from dawn to dark and later. Waters accepted this devotion to duty but failed to go to Bermuda. He then announced that, since he had not gone, there was no reason for cutting the term short.

Peale was indignant. He refused to work out the last four months of his term. There was such wholehearted support of his stand on the part of the neighborhood tradesmen that Waters grudgingly released him from his bond in January, 1762, four months before he became of age.

Charles Willson Peale was a master craftsman and a freeman. Now he and Rachel could marry. He heard wedding bells.

4

Master of Many Trades
Stumbles upon Painting

BEFORE WEDDING bells could ring, the prospective bridegroom had to be able to support a wife. Peale was a craftsman thoroughly trained in his trade, known and liked as an agreeable, well-mannered young man. But in order to set himself up in the saddlery business, he needed capital.

James Tilghman, brother of his godfather, a family friend of the Queen Annes County days, offered a loan of twenty pounds. Elated, Charles ran to Nathan Waters with the news, saying breathlessly that he must go to Norfolk at once to get materials—beechwood, canvas, tools, and the like.

"Why go to Norfolk?" asked Waters. He could let him have enough of his excess materials to get started for only a hundred and fifty pounds.

Peale was flabbergasted. A hundred and fifty pounds! All he had was twenty.

Waters reassured him. He would accept the twenty pounds and a note for the balance. He could pay off the note when he had money to do so. The offer was made with such an air of kindliness, providing a chance to get under way without delay, that Charles forgot all about the trickery of the Bermuda proposal. He signed the note and hurried off to find quarters for his shop. An adequate place, not far from Waters's saddlery on Church Street, was available. The goods from Waters, when delivered, proved not to be what Charles needed. The saddler had got rid of a lot of odds and ends. But it was too late now to protest. The agreement was signed, and he had to make the best of it.

On January 12, 1762, Rachel Brewer, aged sixteen, and Charles Willson Peale, aged twenty, were married. The groom wore one of the suits which Waters had agreed to give him at the end of his indenture, a dark-blue coat and buff knee breeches. Rachel was demure in pale-gray silk; a little bonnet framed her pretty oval face. Wedding bells rang sweetly.

The young people were to live with Mrs. Peale for the present. A home of their own would be obtained when the saddlery began to make money. There was room in the little brick house, for Peale's sister Margaret Jane had married and moved across the bay to Queen Annes County and little Elizabeth had gone to Virginia with her sea-captain husband. Mrs. Peale was glad to have the gaps in the family choir filled.

To give the saddlery a good start, Charles published this announcement in the *Maryland Gazette* of January 21, 1762:

CHARLES WILLSON PEALE, SADDLER
AT HIS SHOP IN CHURCH STREET OVER
AGAINST THE BLACKSMITH'S SHOP
NEAR MR. GASSAWAY'S

HEREBY gives Notice, That he had now set up in his business of Saddlemaking, Polstering and repairing Carriages &c, having proper materials for carrying it on; And will perform any and every part thereof, in the best, neatest and cheapest Manner. And as he is a young man, Just setting out in Business, he hopes to have the employ of his Friends, who may depend on being well and faithfully served by

Their humble servant, CHARLES WILLSON PEALE

The shop was a busy place. Brother James was Charles's right-hand man, for he too was gifted with manual dexterity and quickly learned the craft. Rachel was a useful assistant, performing deftly the tasks assigned to her. The Brewer relatives brought pressure to bear on their friends to patronize the young saddler and orders came in. Peale, ambitious to get ahead rapidly, added side lines which were allied to his craft—upholstering and harness making. He took a chaise maker into partnership, for there was demand for this light, two-wheeled vehicle which looked like a chair with a hood over it. The chaise was serviceable on the rough roads. He increased his knowledge of metalworking so that he could furnish buckles and stirrups for his saddles. Work in brass suggested the desirability of silversmithing. Quickly he mastered that art.

Silver was scarce in North America until the middle of

the nineteenth century. The lack of the precious ore gave
rise to the use of pure silver coins—Spanish, Dutch, or
British—in the manufacture of silverware. Having carefully hoarded money made into ornamental or useful silverware was as good as having it in the bank, especially when
there was no bank. Keeping so much coin out of circulation
resulted in the issuance of paper money. Charles was not
aware that he was contributing to a financial crisis in learning to work silver. It was just another chance to earn money.

Peale's mind was buzzing with plans, and his hands were
never still. Life seemed promising and work was enjoyable
with lovely Rachel at his side. Suddenly a golden light
gleamed over this scene of industry and domestic bliss. A
letter came from a Captain Digby of the British Army
(Digby was a family name). It stated that, if Peale would
come to London at once to present his claim, he would
receive the long-awaited legacy amounting to two thousand pounds. The young saddler was frantic. He could not
leave his newly established business even if he had money
enough to go to London. The only possible action was to
write to a London solicitor, giving all the facts about the
legitimacy of the claim, and ask him to act in his behalf.
Brother St. George, who had inherited his father's gift for
penmanship (but used it to better ends), helped draw up
the letter. No reply came. After months of fruitless waiting, the mirage faded once more.

April, 1762, brought Peale's twenty-first birthday. He
was of age and now legally responsible for debts contracted. Nathan Waters promptly tossed off his sheep's
clothing and appeared as a wolf demanding interest on the
note which Charles had signed. It was a blow. The transac-

28 CHARLES WILLSON PEALE

tion was made with such apparent liberality that Peale
never dreamed that interest would be required. He managed to meet the interest but was sadly disillusioned.

Those dearly bought materials were soon used up, and
Charles went to Norfolk to purchase supplies not obtainable in Annapolis. As the broad-beamed sloop sped down
Chesapeake Bay over a choppy sea, his qualms of seasickness might have been soothed had he known that this journey was to open a new world to him. Not knowing that, he
was entirely miserable. He told of the fateful experience
in his memoirs:

In . . . [Norfolk] he found a brother of Mr Joseph Frazier
who had some fondness for painting and had painted several
landscapes and one Portrait with which he had decorated his
rooms. Had they been better, perhaps they would not have led
Peale into the idea of attempting anything in that way but
rather have smothered that faint spark of genius.

What a challenge to a craftsman who delighted in mastering every technique he undertook. He was familiar with
engravings of paintings but had seen no canvases. His innate good taste told him that Frazier's work was atrocious.
His ambition said, "I can do better than that." And with
that resolution an American painter was born.

The return voyage to Annapolis was made quickly thanks
to favorable wind and tides. But it was hardly fast enough
for Peale, impatient to try his hand at painting. He lost no
time, once he had seen the new supply of materials safely
stowed away in his shop, in getting to work. The chaise
maker had coach paints and brushes; he had canvas in his
shop. Fearlessly he tackled portraiture with Rachel and
James sitting as models. With a mirror ingeniously ar-

ranged, he painted a self-portrait "with a Clock taken to pieces before him." The self-portrait was lost for years but finally turned up in a clutter of materials in his workroom "tied up as a bag and containing a pinch or two of whiting."

Yes, he could do better than Frazier. His first portraits were extravagantly admired by the family, for they were good likenesses. Friends saw them and spread the news of Peale's new accomplishment. Impressed, Colonel Maybury ordered portraits of himself and his wife. Best of all, he paid two pounds for the paintings.

This promised to be a profitable profession and one for which he had a natural inclination. There were some immediate opportunities to use the art of painting. Charles could decorate vehicles with the elaborate coats of arms much in demand at a time when there was a taste for brilliantly colored carriages, sedan chairs, and chaises. He advertised himself as a sign painter. Since few could read, signs for inns and shops set forth their wares in pictorial form. The most alluring signs brought in the best trade.

Coach paints were adequate for such work but were not right for portrait painting. Peale must have materials which were not available in Annapolis; such exotic wares could not be found in a place smaller than Philadelphia. Leaving the saddlery in the care of Rachel, James, and the chaise maker, Charles set out on the long ride to the great city.

The road to Baltimore was fairly good, if a road pitted with holes—some six feet across—can be called good. Peale's sure-footed horse easily avoided these pitfalls; they were less trouble than the numerous gates across the road. On one five-mile stretch near Annapolis Charles counted forty-two gates. As he repeatedly dismounted and remounted, he thought how neatly his father used to sail over gates on his gray hunter. If only his horse had such wings on his feet! Gates or no gates, he made the thirty miles to Baltimore by dusk and lodged at a tavern at the edge of that big, muddy village. Off at dawn the next day, he continued his journey through monotonous, desolate country. Glad of the relief from riding, he ferried across the Susquehanna River at Havre de Grace. Once across, he pushed his tired horse to the utmost to reach a tavern near Elkton. It was hardly more than a grogshop; the food was poor and the bed dirty, but at least there was a good stable for his horse. He rode on relentlessly through the flat, uninteresting countryside, reaching Philadelphia when it was too dark to see what the city looked like. He had ridden the last miles with a Philadelphian who guided him through dimly lit streets, their horses clattering over the new stone pavements that were the pride of Philadelphia. His kind companion left him at the door of a recommended tavern, the Golden Lion. Despite the lateness of the hour, hot food was served to him. Then he stumbled off to bed in a clean, bare dormitory. How good was sleep after the exhausting journey!

In the morning he had a single objective, to find someone who sold painter's materials. The innkeeper directed Charles to a merchant on Chestnut Street whose shop sign bore a golden ball. Before leaving the inn, he inspected its sign critically. Golden Lion, indeed! It looked far more like a cat, and that was precisely what the tavern was called by its clients, the "Yellow Cat."

After the graceful radiating streets of Annapolis, the regular grid of streets crossing each other at right angles looked overly neat, but the stone paving and narrow brick sidewalks were an improvement on the miry streets at home. There were many trees in the city, and a number of the streets bore the names of trees. The Golden Lion was at the corner of Filbert Street, and Charles was now searching for Chestnut and the golden ball. The passers-by seemed soberly dressed compared to the elegantly clothed Marylanders, but he recalled that there were many Quakers in the city. He saw more chaises than carriages on the fine new pavements, and heard the constant clip-clop of horses ridden by substantial-looking gentlemen. Finally Peale found Chestnut Street, and at the corner of Strawberry Lane was a shop whose sign diplayed a shiny, golden ball —Christopher Marshall, Druggist. Some colors and brushes were displayed in the window; he had found what he wanted. Suddenly he felt hesitant about going into the shop. Since he knew only the names of the commonest colors, how could he order? Shrewdly he concealed his ignorance. Boldly striding through the door, he courteously asked Mr. Marshall for a price list of colors so that he could make out a purchasing list to meet his requirements. The shopkeeper gladly gave him a list with prices, and Charles departed, promising to come back to make his purchases in a day or two.

Next he sought a bookshop. Where Front and Market Streets met, Rivington and Brown displayed books in a many-paned bow window. Observing a quiver of goose quills for pens beside the door, Charles made a note to take some back to St. George. In the shop he asked for books on the art of painting. Diligent search unearthed two volumes by Robert Dossie entitled *The Handmaid to the Arts*. Peale bought the books and, clutching his treasure in a firm grip, hurried back to the "Yellow Cat." The sights of the great city beckoned in vain. He hardly took time to eat; slept only when his eyes would no longer stay open; paused only to see that his horse was properly fed; and devoted himself to an intensive study of the *Handmaid*. He learned the names of colors and discovered that they should be ground with linseed oil. Absorbing every scrap of information, he read about brushes, canvas, and varnishes.

When he closed the second volume, he was ready to return to Mr. Marshall's shop. Entering confidently, he ordered what he needed in a professional manner, choosing his materials as if he had long been familiar with such things. When the transaction was completed, Marshall asked Peale if he knew a fellow artist, James Claypoole, who had a painting room not far away. "First Philadelphia-born artist," he explained. "None of these foreign fellows that come over here to make a fortune."

Charles called on Mr. Claypoole at once but did not find him at home. However, a member of his family asked the visitor to come in and showed him portraits that hung in the studio. Claypoole was a man who painted for his own pleasure. His output was not large, but his work was sound and good. Peale looked at the first group of good portraits he had ever seen and learned much from his careful observation. He saw that there was a standard of craftsmanship which he must attain in his work. As he left the painting room—he could have looked at the portraits for hours— he expressed his appreciation for the privilege. He may have caught a glimpse of Claypoole's pretty daughter as he was leaving; she would be his brother James's wife one day.

Charles did not linger. He wanted to return home and

begin his work. He had obtained his painting materials and had seen some fine portraits, but he barely knew what Philadelphia looked like. When he reached the outskirts, he looked back and saw the city rising in a glow of rosy brick between the two rivers, the Delaware and the Schuyl-kill, which bordered it on the east and west. Peale felt a slight pang of regret that he had seen so little and decided that he would return someday.

He paid little attention to the country he rode through; he thought it hardly merited a glance. Lost in dreams of painting, he found the return journey somehow shorter than the trip to Philadelphia. There did not seem to be so many gates between Baltimore and Annapolis. Charles Willson Peale was happy.

The shop was running smoothly, which made it possible for him to devote much of his time to putting his new ideas and tools into practice, but he found there were a number of gaps in his knowledge. How should canvas be prepared so that it would not absorb the paint? Why did the mixture of certain colors produce mud? The *Handmaid* did not tell him these and other things. He must find out.

5

A Son of Liberty
Loses His Liberty

HELP COULD come only from an experienced artist. As far as Peale knew, there were but four men in Maryland at that time who were professional artists. In the early 1700s the South was strangely lacking in the naïve native artists who were portraying the countenances of austere-faced New Englanders and placid burghers of New Amsterdam. Fortunately for Peale, John Hesselius, one of the four Maryland artists, lived just across the Severn from Annapolis. His father, Swedish-born Gustavus Hesselius, had come to America after studying in London with the popular portrait painter, Sir Godfrey Kneller. His fame rested in part on his fine portraits of two Indian chiefs of the Leni-Lenape tribe, which John Penn had asked him to paint as scientific records of Indian types. Gustavus schooled his son well, but John never attained the honest realism of his father's work, though he excelled him in coloring. However, John Hesselius was, for a time, Maryland's leading portraitist, not because he was an outstanding artist but because he had no rival in the field.

Surely a man of so much experience could help Peale solve his problems. Charles approached Hesselius with a proposition. Would he, in exchange for one of Peale's best saddles "complete with furniture," let Peale watch him while he painted a portrait? Hesselius agreed and Charles observed every step in the procedure. First the canvas was stretched on a wooden frame; then it was sized to give it a nonabsorbent surface. When it had dried out, the subject was sketched in charcoal after which the painting in oil colors began. Charles watched with intense interest, not forgetting a detail. When that portrait was finished, Hesselius offered a privilege outside the original bargain. He proposed that he draw a line vertically through a canvas, paint half of a portrait himself, and let Charles finish the other half. The eager student recalled in his memoirs "that these opportunities infinitely lightened the difficulties in a new art with our adventurer."

Our adventurer now asked everyone he met if he knew anyone who had a portrait in his home? Many of the wealthy landowners had brought family portraits with them from England. Peale spared no pains in his effort to inspect every painting he heard about, often riding many miles to a distant plantation. He never passed the State House without stopping to study a portrait of Lord Baltimore by Kneller, a gift to Maryland from Queen Anne. Charles was determined to be a really good artist and eagerly sought every means of attaining that goal. Everything seemed propitious for his mastering the technique of painting and succeeding in portraiture as a profession.

Fate intervened to disrupt such progress. Great grief came to Rachel and Charles, the death of their first-born, a daughter, after twelve days of feeble existence. Nathan Waters chose that time to press Peale for payment of the money he owed for the saddlery materials. His demand came when there was no money at all. The chaise-maker partner had just decamped, taking with him the cash on hand. He also owed Charles money.

In desperation he made another attempt to learn something about the legacy. This time he enlisted the legal aid of Charles Carroll, the Barrister. One of the wealthiest and wittiest of the Maryland aristocrats, Carroll was a brilliant lawyer. He sent copies of the records of Peale's birth and the marriage of his parents with a summation of all available information about the legacy to a reliable solicitor in London, asking him to investigate. Months passed, and no answer was received. Carroll sent duplicates, but for some reason never disclosed, neither inquiry brought a reply.

Knowing that he could not depend on capturing the illusive will-o'-the-wisp, Peale sought concrete means of raising money. He offered his stock of saddles and harness at bargain prices, but that was hardly profitable. Opportunely, a Scottish gentleman came along with a stock of imperfect watches he had bought as a gamble and asked Peale to put them in working condition. A demand for this self-taught craft gave Peale an idea, and he inserted a notice in the *Maryland Gazette:*

CHARLES WILLSON PEALE

At his shop in Church Street, ANNAPOLIS

Makes, Cleans and Repairs CLOCKS, and Cleans and Mends Watches, in the best, neatest and cheapest Manner and with the Greatest Expedition. Any

Gentleman who shall be pleased to Employ him,
may depend on being faithfully served by,
    Their humble servant, CHARLES WILLSON PEALE

N.B. He likewise carries on the Saddlery Business
in all its branches as heretofore.

When William Knapp, the Annapolis watchmaker, read
this notice, he exploded with indignation. He was "reg-
ularly bred to the watchmaking business and had had instruction from the most eminent in London and Dublin
in that way." Was Charles Peale with no professional training to take the bread out of the mouth of an established
practitioner?

Evidently not. Charles retreated, leaving the field to the
protesting Mr. Knapp. Resourceful and indefatigable, he
tried out a way of making use of all his skills. Packing
a two-wheeled cart with saddles and harnesses, watches
and clocks, tools and necessary materials, including paints
and brushes, he traveled from plantation to plantation to
solicit work. He mended saddles and gear, repaired time-
pieces, painted coats of arms or portraits as requested, and
wrought silver when someone had a hoard of coins to use
for that purpose.

Coin to pay Charles was another matter. There was a
good market for his services, but money was scarce. Landowners were accustomed to barter tobacco and other produce for necessities. And Charles needed real money.

These admirable attempts, which brought such meager
results, convinced Charles that there was only one course
for him to follow and that was to devote his entire time to
portrait painting. There was little competition, and it was

fairly certain that those rich enough to order portraits would have money to pay for them. The decision was pleasing to Peale. He knew that painting was work for which he had talent and inclination. Later he was to write, "Looking back Peale saw only good in those hardships for they forced him to devote himself particularly to painting and make every effort to excell in that art."

But he was not yet able to devote himself wholly to painting. Patriotism was making demands on his time and his emotions. Peale had recently joined the Sons of Liberty, a group of young men who pledged themselves to fight the growing tyranny of British rule. Annapolis, as a busy seaport, felt the weight of the taxes which England was imposing on shipping and imports. Resentment was growing among her liberal citizens who were on the lookout for means of publicly expressing their feelings against the Loyalist, pro-British, domination in local government.

A campaign then under way for a seat in the provincial assembly gave the liberals a chance to demonstrate their opposition to the Loyalists. They put up a people's candidate, young Samuel Chase. Chase was a lawyer of Peale's age and seemed to that artisan and tradesman a valiant champion of the rank and file of the citizenry. He entered the campaign for Chase with ardent enthusiasm.

Answering a knock at his door, he was greeted by a group of fellow Sons of Liberty. "You know how to paint, Charly," they said. "Make us some good banners to carry in our parades. Nice big letters so people can read."

Charles was ready to help. "What shall I put on the banners?"

They all had suggestions: "Samuel Chase the People's

Candidate," "Elect Sam Chase and Protect the Rights of Tradesmen," "Down with the Crown Courts," or similar sentiments. "Bring them to the Liberty Tree tonight for the rally," they called as they were leaving.

Charles dropped his current task and applied himself to making effective banners. He carried the banners to the great tulip poplar near King William's School under which the liberals were holding a noisy demonstration for Samuel Chase and against his opponent George Stuart. At the end of the meeting, holding Peale's banners high and shouting the slogans, they all paraded through the streets.

At the height of the bitter campaign, Rachel was coming from the fish market with her basket filled with the delicious seafood so cheap and abundant in Annapolis, when a strange woman drew abreast of her and in a low voice said, "Tell your husband he's goin' to get in sore trouble if he keeps on fightin' for Chase."

Rachel was startled. "Mr. Peale knows Mr. Chase is a good man and is going to help plain folks to get their rights. What is wrong about that?"

"Right or wrong is no matter. Them as he owes money to is goin' to harm him. Tell him to heed." She slipped quietly down a side street.

Much troubled, Rachel repeated this warning to Charles. The threat of danger served only to inflame his ardor, and he continued to play a prominent part in the campaign.

The unexpected happened. Samuel Chase was elected to the assembly! This break in their hitherto undisputed power infuriated the Loyalists, and they determined to take revenge on all who had publicly supported Chase.

Charles Willson Peale, poor and heavily in debt, not because of extravagance but through the overextension of his business enterprises, was a sitting duck for their shots. Four Loyalist creditors had writs served on Peale, threatening arrest unless the debts were paid at once.

He went to his friend Isaac Harris for counsel. They went over his affairs carefully. His assets were three hundred pounds in collectable bills and the stock and tools of his trade. On the other side of the ledger, he owed nine hundred pounds. Harris looked grave.

"You cannot possibly meet those demands, Charles, and you will be in jail before you know it. Leave Annapolis at once. I will do what I can with your assets. Meanwhile go to some place where you can earn money with your painting."

Charles's face lighted at the word painting. He said his sister Margaret Jane had written that a neighbor would like to have portraits of his family painted by Peale. He and Rachel could visit his sister at Tuckahoe Bridge across the bay. Her husband kept an inn and could accommodate them easily.

"Excellent," said Harris, "but go tonight."

Hastily, while Rachel gathered together a few belongings, Peale packed the all-important painting box and rolled up some canvas. It was bitterly hard to be forced to leave the home which his wise and loving mother had made so pleasant for them during the past three years. To avoid suspicion on the part of neighbors, James nonchalantly carried the painting box away from the house; somewhat later, St. George strolled out with a bundle of clothing. As dusk fell on that spring night of 1765, Charles and Rachel slipped away, taking only enough money to pay their boat fare

across the bay; everything else was left for the creditors.
At the ferry wharf the brothers waited with the baggage.
Despite heavy hearts the farewells were outwardly cheerful as they boarded the boat. It was so chilly that they were
forced to take refuge in one of the tiny cabins of the ferry,
where they tried to sleep on the narrow wooden shelves
called "bunks."

The next day, in Queen Annes County where Peale had
been born, they were welcomed at the inn by Margaret
Jane's husband, James McMordia. Margaret Jane came running to greet them. "You have come to paint the portraits,"
she called happily. Her gay mood quickly faded, however,
when they told the more imperative reason for their coming.

Peale would have liked to paint his attractive sister first
of all. Her rich auburn hair, deep blue eyes, and beautifully modeled lips made a perfect subject. But practical
matters came first, and he started without delay the portraits which Margaret Jane's neighbor, Captain Cole, had
ordered. Soon finished, they were highly appreciated—
Peale had a happy faculty for catching likenesses—and
Captain Cole paid Charles promptly. It was an auspicious
beginning, and he looked about for other commissions.
Things looked brighter for the fugitives.

Meanwhile the news of Peale's arrival in Queen Annes
County reached James Tilghman, who had started Charles
in his saddlery business with a loan of twenty pounds.
Charles had paid no interest on the loan and had neglected
to get in contact with Tilghman to let him know how matters stood with him at present. Tilghman was hurt by
Charles's remissness. In addition, as a staunch Loyalist, he

had strongly resented Peale's support of Sam Chase in the recent election. Thoroughly angry, he had a writ issued for Charles's arrest.

One day while Peale was absorbed in watching the mechanics of a tidal mill near the inn—when the tide came in, the wheel turned one way; as it went out, it reversed—McMordia ran to him with the news that he must leave at once. A friend had just informed him about the writ, which would be served in a few hours. While Charles gathered up his painting materials and a few essentials of clothing, McMordia, with some of the money received from Captain Cole, purchased a mare named Gimlet for him. This time Charles had to get across the line into Virginia and take refuge with his sister Elizabeth, who now lived in Accomac County.

It was a hard parting for Charles and Rachel, so devotedly in love with each other. It was especially sad because they were expecting their second child. Margaret Jane promised to care tenderly for Rachel and pushed Charles out the door. Off he galloped with the big painting box strapped behind the saddle. Rachel watched through her tears until he was hidden by a grove of pines, hoping that he would get far away before his flight was discovered.

Charles rode rapidly along the sandy forest trails, which were paths formerly used by the Indians. He hoped that the streams along the way would be shallow enough to ford, for he could not risk using ferries. The first day he did not stop for food. Later he halted briefly at a cottage off the trail, where he was generously offered a simple meal.

For three days he rode, pausing in lonely places to let Gimlet graze and to snatch a bit of rest. The woods were musical with bird song. He found comfort in the cheerful warbling but dared not take time to look for the songsters among the branches. The painting box had worn a great raw spot on Gimlet's flank. Tired and disheartened, Peale gave way to a fit of temper, emptied the painting kit of brushes and colors, which he crammed into the saddlebags and threw the heavy box away.

It was a relief to reach the Virginia line and know he was safe from pursuit. He could now safely ask hospitality at the plantations along the way. But a new discomfort came to plague him, a violently aching tooth. At the house where he stopped for the night, he was advised to chew tobacco to ease the pain. He tried it, and the tobacco made him so deathly ill that the toothache was not noticeable.

On the sixth miserable, weary day he reached the home of his sister Elizabeth and her sea-captain husband, Robert Polk. They were so glad to see him, so distressed at his plight, that he was soothed and comforted. Above all he knew that he was secure.

Gimlet, cropping contentedly in the pasture, also was glad to have come to journey's end. The sore on her flank was healing nicely.

6

Journey to the North

ROBERT POLK owned a small coasting vessel, which was being loaded with a cargo of grain the day Peale arrived. He was taking it to northern ports, and when it was ready to sail, he asked Charles if he would like to go with him. It would give him a chance to see something of New England, and he could be of real help on the ship. Charles was only too glad to go. There was nothing for him to do in the little port, and he welcomed an opportunity to be useful to his brother-in-law.

The voyage was uneventful, the summer winds were favorable, and Charles found to his relief that it was possible to be at sea and yet not be seasick. All went well and Polk was able to write in his log, "In Seven Days arrive at Boston the Metropelis of New England." It was now the third week of August, 1765.

They tied up at Clark's Wharf on a Sunday, and the stillness of a Puritan Sabbath lay over Boston. Had they arrived on a weekday, the wharf would have been alive with activity and enlivened by shows of various kinds—tumblers, acrobats, trained animals, with an occasional performance by a troupe of wandering players. But now silence reigned and with it a symphony of smells. The fragrance of spices from warehouses along the shore mingled with the pungent tarry aroma of ropes and rigging in the ship-chandlers' shops, and the strong odors of fish and harbor water.

In their southern innocence Charles and Robert wished to stretch their legs after a week's confinement on the little ship. But they were stopped; Boston blue laws forbade strolling on Sunday except to and from religious worship. There was nothing to do but wait patiently for Monday. Charles occupied himself with making a sketch but found his painting materials sadly inadequate after the painting-box episode. He decided to seek out a color dealer the next day.

On Monday the "Metropelis" was an amazing contrast to the hush of the previous day. Along the water front, vessels of all sizes were either loading or discharging freight in an uproar of shouts, nautical oaths, and the squealing of hundreds of pulleys. Carts clattered over the rough cobblestones; the narrow streets were thronged with bustling Bostonians, so different from the leisurely inhabitants of Annapolis. The buildings of various sizes and shapes and the irregular tangle of streets made Charles appreciative in retrospect of Philadelphia's red-brick uniformity and the geometric crisscross of her shaded streets.

Polk had to remain on the vessel to interview prospective buyers of his freight. Peale wandered along through the maze of streets, seeking only one thing—a dealer in painting materials. At last he found a shop which offered such goods. The Scottish proprietor, John Moffatt, showed a friendly interest in his customer. After a discussion of the

purchases Peale wished to make, Moffatt invited him to
see some paintings by his uncle John Smibert.

Naturally Charles was all eagerness, and they climbed
up ladderlike stairs to a room in which the walls were covered with green baize. Against this background were
displayed copies of European paintings, partially finished
portraits, and sketches of classical subjects. This work was
superior to anything which Peale had seen previously. The
copies of Italian masterpieces were a revelation to him.
Here were some of the works he knew through the engravings he had copied in his youth. To see them in all the glory
of color was thrilling.

Peale wanted to know about John Smibert. His nephew
was only too pleased to give the visitor a brief sketch of his
distinguished uncle's career. He began as a house painter
in Scotland and later went to London to be a painter of
coaches. There he obtained some lessons in portrait painting from Sir Godfrey Kneller. Following that, he traveled
in Italy, where he copied a large number of Italian masterpieces. He came to America in 1728 at the request of Bishop
Berkeley, of Boston, who wanted him to found a college
of arts and sciences for the inhabitants of Bermuda. This
plan came to nothing, and Smibert settled in Boston, painting portraits of most of the eminent clergymen and magis-
trates of New England and their families. His first subject
was Bishop Berkeley surrounded by his family. In 1730 he
staged what was probably the first art exhibition in America, showing his collection of copies. The exhibition was
received with enthusiasm and even inspired a long poem.

At this point Smibert's nephew paused, went to a desk at
one side of the room, and rummaged about until he found

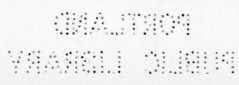

the poem. He read it aloud, laying particular emphasis on
these lines:

> *Still wondrous Artist let thy pencil flow*
> *Still warm with life, thy blended colors glow.*
> *Raise the ripe blush, bid the quick eyeballs roll,*
> *And call forth every passion of the soul.*

Would someone write a poem about his painting one
day, Peale wondered, as he was left alone in the baize-
lined room to study and admire the paintings. He always
learned much from such observation, setting new standards
for himself from each good painting he saw.

He tore himself away at last and descended to the shop,
which originally had belonged to John Smibert. Following
the custom of artists of that time, he had sold painting supplies as an adjunct to his studio. The same slave who had
ground colors for Smibert now performed the task for his
nephew. He had finished preparing Charles's order, and
thanking Mr. Moffatt for his kindness, Peale started back
to Clark's Wharf. He was so immersed in dreams that he
lost his way several times. His head was full of saints and
goddesses and beauty of color.

When Peale finally reached the vessel, Polk was full of
news. There had been riots in Boston on August 14, a wild
protest against the Stamp Act which was to go into effect
in November.

All New England was seething with revolt against the
Stamp Act which the British Parliament had voted to im-
pose on the colonies. Britain needed money after the seven-
year war with France by which she gained possession of
Canada. She felt that the expense of colonial administra-

tion should be met by taxation of the colonies but neglected to take full account of their feelings in the matter. Holland and parts of England had raised funds successfully by means of the sale of stamped paper. If applied to the colonies, it would spread taxation over seaboard and inland colonies alike. Parliament, therefore, decreed that stamped paper must be used for all legal papers, bonds, bills, licenses, deeds, and policies, as well as parchment and paper for documents and newspapers.

Britain was unprepared for the storm raised by the announcement of taxation in this form. The colonists saw that British tax agents would have their noses in every business transaction; they were too independent to tolerate that. They believed that they had done their share in supplying money, volunteer troops, and supplies to aid the British in the French war. Was this harsh measure the reward for the help which the colonists had so willingly given? The greatest cause for resentment lay in the fact that these taxes were imposed by a body in which the colonies had no voice. They would not submit to taxation without representation.

Benjamin Franklin, agent for Pennsylvania in London, who was also authorized to represent some of the other colonies, protested in their behalf. If left to themselves, the colonists would be willing to raise monies for the treasury, but they could not be coerced. His protest had no effect, and the decree became law.

August and September saw violent demonstrations against the act in Boston. There were many unemployed workers, caught in the slump which followed the end of the French war, now that there was no longer a market for military supplies. These men, ripe for revolt, expressed their personal discontent in public protests against the hated decree.

Polk told Peale that on August 14 there had been tremendous riots. Effigies of Andrew Oliver, the Royal Stamp Distributor, were carried through the streets, hung, and burned. The crowd, inflamed by both patriotism and rum, had looted and destroyed, getting entirely out of hand. That ardent Son of Liberty, Peale, regretted that he had not arrived in Boston a little earlier. He would have loved joining a rally under Boston's Liberty Tree and sharing the roused feelings of the Bostonians.

He would have liked to stay longer in Boston, but since he had no money, he had to go on with Polk in order to have board and shelter. Polk intended to sail up the coast to Newburyport, where he had a purchaser for the remainder of his cargo. It was a stormy voyage along the rocky coast, and Charles was glad indeed when they anchored in Newburyport Harbor. As they were to remain in harbor for some time, Polk asked Peale to paint the outside of the vessel. Peale tackled the work willingly and made, as he did with everything, a good workmanlike job of it.

When the craft was gleaming and shipshape, Peale was free to turn to higher manifestations of the art of painting and try out some of the ideas he had gleaned from Smibert's paintings. He started with a self-portrait, which was admirably successful. It was hung in the ship's cabin where merchants who came to deal with Polk saw it. One prosperous merchant liked it so much that he asked Peale to paint likenesses of his three children. Later he received a commission to "paint a Lady" as well. The sides of his purse were rounding out in a gratifying manner.

Evenings were spent ashore with Sons of Liberty in New-buryport. They were holding, almost daily, meetings of protest against the Stamp Act. Peale's talents with a brush were discovered, and the demonstrators begged him to paint some banners for their parades. He felt quite at home with banners now. Here, too, effigies of Oliver were hung and burned. Fragments rescued from the flames were stamped upon with loud cries of "Stamp him! Stamp him!" Charles and Polk joined the demonstrations and shouted disapproval of the Stamp Act with gusto but with a southern accent.

How elated they would have been if they could have foreseen that when November came no agents would be on hand to distribute the stamped paper; they had resigned or fled. The act could not be enforced, and in March, 1766, it was repealed by Parliament. Ostensibly it was a gracious move on the part of the government, but in reality an action was forced by the whirlwind of revolt raised in the colonies and by the crippling boycott of British goods.

Peale now had a little money in his purse, which made it possible to return to Boston. Polk approved of his going and loaned him sixteen pounds to add to what he had earned from painting portraits. Bidding his brother-in-law an affectionate farewell, Charles returned to the "Metropelis" of New England.

7

Lessons from Copley: Virginian Hospitality

WHEN PEALE reached Boston, his first concern was to find inexpensive lodgings. In making inquiries about inns, he learned by chance that the proprietor of the Exchange Tavern was looking for someone to teach his son drawing. Charles wasted no time; he fairly ran to the tavern. Blodget, the innkeeper, made a bargain with him. For two Spanish dollars and lessons for his son, he would provide board and lodging. Since the name of Blodget does not appear in the annals of art, it may be assumed that Peale's pupil was no genius.

As soon as he was settled in his clean little attic room at the tavern, Charles revisited Moffatt, the amiable color merchant. He hoped that Moffatt would be able to help him secure some portrait commissions; he needed an income sorely.

Moffatt was willing to be helpful but feared he could do nothing for him. There was, in Boston, an artist who was so popular and so sought after that he had a monopoly of the portrait business. Prominent Bostonians and those of lesser importance who wanted to be painted had to make appointments weeks or even months in advance. Anyone who objected was told he could take it or leave it. This painter had more work than he could possibly cope with.

Peale interrupted the flow of information. "Who is this important artist?"

"His name is John Singleton Copley." Moffatt was struck with an idea. "Why not call on him? He might give you some of the orders he has to refuse."

Charles curbed his impatient desire to rush off at once to meet this remarkable person. But he wanted to hear more about him, and Moffatt seemed to be a mine of information.

Copley's father had died before John was born, and his mother supported herself and her child by keeping a tobacco shop on Long Wharf, the center of commercial activity in Boston. The teeming throng of merchants, seamen, buyers, and hucksters, which crowded the wharf, bought "the best Tobacco, cut, pigtail and spun" from the widow.

When John was ten years old, his mother married Peter Pelham, an English painter and mezzotint engraver. In England, Pelham had a profitable business selling his engraved reproductions of paintings, especially the portraits of British notables. In the pre-photographic era there were popular demand and wide market for these inexpensive prints. The humblest home could decorate its walls with portraits of titled ladies or political bigwigs. When Pelham came to America, hoping to build up a similar business, he discovered there were no paintings to reproduce. He was forced to paint a portrait of some well-known person to provide himself with a subject for an engraving. To eke out his earnings in this field, he gave lessons in "dancing, reading, painting on glass and all sorts of needlework."

John pored over a portfolio of engravings which Pelham had brought from England. When Pelham discovered the boy trying to copy some of them, he gave him lessons in drawing, painting in oil, and in the delicate technique of painting miniatures on ivory. Pelham found that he had an exceptionally talented pupil. John made such strides in his work that at the age of thirteen he began his career as a professional portrait painter.

"Lucky for the boy that his mother married an artist; he could be learning every minute of the day," observed Moffatt.

At twenty, Copley was head and shoulders above the few painters who were working in Boston. Now at twenty-seven——

Charles exclaimed at that. "Only three years older than I am, and he has made such a success of his work! Where is his painting room?"

It was in a breezy loft over Mrs. Pelham's tobacco shop. A fine view of the tangle of masts in Boston Harbor could be seen from its windows. Peale was announced and was most cordially received by Copley, who ordinarily was diffident and reserved.

Peale thought he looked like a prosperous shopkeeper— his figure was stocky and without grace—but he was handsomely dressed in a rich maroon coat. He graciously showed Peale the portraits, completed or partially painted, which were in his painting room. Peale liked the colors he used, cool greens, russets, tans, and grays, and admired the solidity of his figures. Years later he recorded that "the Sight of Mr Copley's picture rooms was a great feast to Peale."

Never timid where his career was concerned, Peale had the courage to ask Copley to give him instruction in painting. Copley was willing and invited Charles to come to the studio and copy one of his paintings. He gave him lessons in miniature painting, for he told Peale that miniatures were much in demand and profitable. Copley was amazed to see how quickly he mastered that meticulous technique. The disciplined eye and the hand of a trained craftsman were great assets.

Just to be in Copley's painting room was instructive. His concentration was so complete that absolute silence reigned while he painted. He was tense and worked slowly. Peale liked to watch him mix a flesh tone, then take a sample over to the sitter, and compare it with the actual skin color. He was merciless with his sitters. Often they had to pose for six hours at a stretch with only brief rest periods.

Peale took notes on Copley's scale of prices, which he quoted as definitely as would any shopkeeper. They were graded as follows:

The price of Whole Lengths, 40 guineas; half-length, 20; one-fourth pieces or busts, 10; Wether Men or Women makes no difference in price, nor does Dress, but Children in the one-fourth pieces will be more because of the addition of hands which must be when a child is put in that size, (which is not the case with grown people,) but should the hands be omitted, the picture may be smaller and then the price will be the same as for a Mans or Womans without hands.

Though Peale received several orders for miniatures through Copley, his funds were getting low. He sold his faithful watch for five pounds. A portrait commission brought him twelve Spanish dollars. It was clear to Peale that he could not make a living as an artist in Boston; the competition from Copley was too strong. He must get back to the South where he would have better opportunities; moreover, he could not endure separation from Rachel any longer. There must be a child by now. In a chance conversation with a captain on the Long Wharf, he was offered free passage to Virginia on a vessel that was to sail the next day.

Charles hurriedly visited Moffatt to lay in a good stock of materials; then he called to bid farewell to Copley. He boarded the Virginia-bound vessel which immediately ran into a terrific storm and miraculously escaped shipwreck on treacherous rocks. The sound of the anchor rattling down into the waters of Metempkin Inlet in Virginia was pleasant music to Peale, the seasick passenger.

No sooner had they anchored than a small boat put out from shore bringing a visitor who clambered up the rope ladder to the deck. The captain led him into the cabin where Peale's self-portrait was hanging, the same painting that had been admired by visitors on Polk's ship. It at once caught the eye of James Arbuckle who asked who had painted it. Peale, pale and wan, was brought to the cabin and presented. The two men took an instant liking to one another.

Handsome, hearty Arbuckle, with southern impetuosity, invited Peale ashore as his guest. He wanted him to paint his own and "his Ladys and Childs" portraits, and he felt confident that there would be many commissions from his friends.

It seemed an excellent professional opening, and Peale accepted the invitation gladly. He might earn enough money to satisfy some of his creditors at home. He collected his belongings, tucked the lucky self-portrait under his arm (which made his descent into the shore boat hazardous), and accompanied Arbuckle to his comfortable mansion on a thriving plantation. Mrs. Arbuckle welcomed the attractive, cultivated guest, a godsend to their dull country existence. When she found that he was musical and loved to sing, she was overjoyed, for she and her husband were ardent music lovers.

Peale settled down to an agreeable life, luxuriously housed, lavishly fed, with abundant time for painting. His portraits of the family received high praise, and Peale's reputation as a fine portraitist spread through the countryside. When not actually engaged in filling the orders which came in, he experimented constantly, putting into practice what he had learned from Copley. He had made notable gains in technique; he had a firmer control of color and there was added grace in the arrangement of his composition.

A common love for mechanics formed a bond between Arbuckle and Peale. Arbuckle was constructing a violin. Fascinated by the acoustic problems, Peale tried to play another fiddle which Arbuckle had but drew from it only ear-piercing wails. To amuse his host, Charles taught him the rudiments of clock and watch repairing. There were no watchmakers in that region, and when word got around that Peale was an expert in this field, he was overwhelmed with requests for repair work. It might have been profitable, but Peale felt that returning to a craft would be detri-

mental to his progress as a professional painter. He refused
the work as well as Arbuckle's offer to build a house for
him on the plantation. James Arbuckle wanted to keep this
delightful companion near him.

Peale longed to return to Annapolis, to his beloved
wife, to see the child born during his absence, and to be
reunited with his mother and brothers. Unconsciously he
prepared the way for his return by sending two gifts to
Annapolis. One, a recent painting, was sent to John Bordley. The other, his color interpretation of an engraving of
a portrait by Sir Joshua Reynolds, went to Charles Carroll,
the Barrister.

Carroll was immensely impressed by the technical excellence and beauty of the painting he received from Peale.
It seemed to him a pity that so gifted a citizen should be
exiled from Annapolis. Enlisting the penmanship of St.
George Peale, now principal clerk in the land office of
Maryland, he drew up letters granting Peale four years'
indulgence from his debts. These were signed by all his
creditors except the four stubborn Loyalists.

When word reached Charles of this effort in his behalf,
he decided to risk the incomplete immunity and return to
Annapolis. After six happy months with the warmhearted
Arbuckles, Peale left with great regret. It had been an important period in his artistic development, for he had had
leisure, free from distraction, for his work. He had thus
been able to establish his individual style, and consolidate
what he had learned from others in his technique.

The reunion with his family was deliriously happy. Rachel seemed to have gained in beauty, and his son James
was a child far superior to other babies. Margaret Peale

beamed with pride on this son of hers, now an accomplished artist. She wished his father could have shared her pride.

Peale's joy was short-lived. The four implacable creditors threatened arrest if they were not paid. To come home only to face an open door to prison was cruel indeed. Fortunately, Rachel received an inheritance at this time. The creditors accepted this as security, and Peale was free to take up his life in Annapolis.

Requests for portraits came in as the news got about that Peale had returned, and his reputation as a competent painter grew rapidly. When he had free time, he gave his brother James lessons in miniature painting, for James had a definite artistic gift. A pleasant, prosperous period seemed to lie ahead, and Peale was content with his lot.

Out of a clear sky came the startling consequences of the gift he had sent John Bordley from Virginia, a painting which was to change the course of his life.

8

Peale Goes to London

JOHN BORDLEY was now a provincial judge and a member of the Governor's Council. Returning to Annapolis one evening after an official trip, too late to cross the bay to his new estate on Wye Island off the Eastern Shore, he decided to spend the night at his sister's home, where he was always welcome. Elizabeth Bordley greeted him with the news that a gift from Charly Peale was awaiting him in the storeroom. Bordley wanted to unpack it at once, but Elizabeth shooed him off to bed. It was late and he was tired. "It will be there in the morning," she promised.

As soon as it grew light the next morning, without waiting to get fully dressed "nor even his stockings gartered up," he unwrapped his present in the unheated storeroom. Two hours later, goose-pimpled and shivering, he emerged to seek the comfort of a crackling fire. Oblivious to the October cold, he had spent the time in rapt examination of Peale's painting, for having become a good amateur painter himself, he could appreciate the niceties of painting technique. Elizabeth looked at her brother with kindly amusement as he warmed himself before the fire, his stockings

down around his ankles, his florid face a deeper pink than
usual, and his fine gray eyes shining with excitement.

"Peale has made wonderful progress," he told his sister.
"Something must and shall be done for him."

Bordley lost no time in putting that resolve into action.
He wrote a letter to Charles Carroll in which he offered to
donate ten guineas toward a fund to finance a year's study
of art in London for Charles. Would Carroll help?

Carroll, who had already demonstrated his admiration
for Peale as an artist by his aid in the matter of Peale's debts,
agreed to contribute five guineas. In addition he laid the
matter before the Governor's Council, using this argument:
Britain was aware of Maryland's superior commercial
standing. Would it not be well to draw attention to her cultural atmosphere as well? What better means to that end
than to give a gifted native son a chance to develop his
talents to the full? The achievements of a great artist would
redound to the glory of Maryland.

Cries of "Hear! Hear!" and applause greeted these words,
and the council, led by Governor Sharpe who gave eight
pounds, brought the total of the fund up to eighty-three
pounds. With careful management that would pay for the
voyage and for a year's stay in London. All took it for
granted that Peale would study with Benjamin West, the
Philadelphia Quaker youth who was so brilliantly successful in England. The Barrister secured a letter of introduction to West from William Allen, one of the Philadelphia
merchants who had financed West's study of painting in
Italy. Bordley wrote presenting Peale to his stepfather
Edmond Jenings, in London, and the Barrister commended
the young man to his London agent in these terms:

The bearer hereof, Charles Willson Peale, a young man of this town has a turn for Limning and some other Branches of Painting. He likewise has Pretensions to an Interest in Oxfordshire. As his circumstances are but low, I am willing to advance 20 or 25 guineas to Enable him to take this trip to England to see what he can make of his Pretensions and to get some further insight into the Profession.

Carroll wanted Charles to get to the root of that illusive inheritance once and for all.

Meanwhile the object of all this kindness was suffering conflicting emotions. Charles was eager to avail himself of this splendid chance to obtain greater mastery of painting techniques and to acquire the prestige which study abroad would give him. But he found it hard to leave Rachel and the baby and to abandon the portrait commissions which were beginning to come his way. His good sense, however, convinced him that greater success as an artist would mean a brighter future for his family. He accepted the generosity of Bordley and the council with deep gratitude, promising to repay them in portraits when he returned to Annapolis.

A piece of luck hastened his departure. Bales of stamped paper had been stored for nearly a year in the hold of a British vessel standing off Annapolis. The repeal of the Stamp Act made it useless, and Governor Sharpe ordered the paper transferred to the ship *Brandon* for its return to England. Peale was offered free passage on the *Brandon*, leaving his fund intact until he reached London.

The day of Peale's departure in mid-December, 1766, was dark and stormy, a fitting atmosphere for parting from Rachel and his little boy. The whole family went to see him embark. Mrs. Peale wept bitterly, while his brothers made facetious comments to hide their feelings. Rachel bravely kept back the tears, telling herself that Charly's great opportunity outweighed her loss of his companionship.

The *Brandon* danced down the choppy waters of the bay very prettily, but she met terrific winter gales in the Atlantic and for days could spread no more than a handkerchief of sail. Charles took to his bunk in the cramped, airless cabin, tossed back and forth, up and down, desperately seasick, terrified by the ominous sounds of creaking timbers and the rigging screaming in the gale. Once the laboring vessel shipped a mountainous sea which broke the skylight above Peale's cabin, drenching him and all his possessions in a deluge of icy salt water. It was bitter cold, and the dampness penetrated his very bones. What with chickens and pigs aboard for fresh meat, cooking aromas, and the stench of bilge, the *Brandon* was a veritable Pandora's box of vile smells which assailed the stricken passenger and caused fresh qualms.

The storm abated for a few days, and sunshine sparkled on the cold blue of the ocean. Charles recovered his equilibrium sufficiently to visit the ship's carpenter, a friendly soul who loaned Peale tools and provided seasoned wood for a project Peale had thought up as he lay in his bunk. Charles recalled what he had learned from James Arbuckle about the construction of a violin and now was determined to make a fiddle. What he used for strings is not known; it is hoped that the ship's cat survived. While the final result was not a Stradivarius, it did produce sounds. He scraped a tune or two from it for the amusement of the ship's company. This inspired Captain McLachlan to try his hand on it, and a squeaky but lively version of a good jig, "Logan's Water," set some dancing feet in motion.

After this peaceful interlude fresh storms blew up, and Charles returned to his cabin and his miseries. He was in no mood for music then. The voyage, of almost unrelieved rough weather, lasted eight weeks, and all aboard rejoiced when the *Brandon* edged into the mouth of the Thames. As she approached London, Charles could only liken the density of masts at the docks to a forest of bare trees. He stepped ashore on February 13, 1767, staggered weakly to a hackney chaise, and was driven to an inn recommended by the captain. The roar and tumult of the streets dizzied him into queasiness, and he shut his eyes to the animated scene, longing only for a quiet world that would stop heaving up and down.

When he had had some hours of rest, Charles asked at the inn where he could buy fresh clothes—his were sadly water-stained. At the tailor's shop he selected a costume to his liking, for Peale had a touch of vanity in his make-up and a love for fine clothes. "A half-dress suit of pale blue, a beaver hat, shoes and black stockings" were delivered by the tailor the next day, and Peale felt presentable enough to offer his introduction to Benjamin West. He reviewed what he knew about West, feeling a surge of patriotic pride in this fellow American.

West was a self-taught Quaker who did his first painting with brushes made of cat's hair, using earth colors obtained from the Indians. His talent was so striking that a group of Philadelphia merchants agreed, "It is a pity that such genius should be cramped for the want of a little cash," and donated sufficient money to enable West to go to Italy to study painting. In Rome, falling under the spell of classical art forms, Roman mythology, and history, he produced work under that inspiration which won praise from fellow artists. From Rome he went to London for a visit and remained for the rest of his life. In the beginning he made his living painting portraits, but his heart was set on doing vast canvases depicting classical incidents. Luckily for him, the Archbishop of York became interested in West's work through his love for the classics. The Archbishop suggested a theme for a composition—"Agrippina with the Ashes of Germanicus"—and when the painting was completed, invited George III to see it and to meet the young colonial artist. The king considered himself a connoisseur of art, had begun a collection of Italian and Dutch paintings, and now was taking an interest in British painters. This interest was most valuable to the hitherto neglected native artists.

West was summoned to the royal palace and on arrival was ushered into a room where the king would receive him. With the help of a footman, he set up the canvas in a good light. Plump King George bustled in, looked carefully at the painting, and then, to West's relief, his pudgy face lighted with a smile and his prominent eyes sparkled with pleasure. He had spied a Doric temple in the background, and the king's favorite order of architecture was the Doric. Delighted with this coincidence, he turned to inspect the artist to whom he took an instant liking. There was another coincidence; they were exactly of an age! King George promptly commissioned West to do a painting on the subject of the "Departure of Regulus from Rome," and a long, close friendship ensued between king and artist. West was given a studio in the palace and was appointed Court His-

torical Painter. His future was assured. It was odd that a
Quaker boy, born to a creed of simplicity and humility,
should become the darling of British court circles, delight-
ing their taste with his pompous, pretentious canvases.
Philadelphia was far, far away.

No matter how glittering his worldly position or how
spectacular his artistic success, Benjamin West was always
ready to welcome young countrymen aspiring to an artist's
career and to aid them in achieving their ambition. Small
wonder that he was called "a Gibraltar of kindness to American artists and pupils."

Toward this "Gibraltar" Charles Willson Peale made his
way in a sedan chair, moving by inches in the narrow,
crowded streets amid the prodigious din of clattering
hoofs, cracking whips, and raucous shouts of chair bearers
asking for way in pungent terms. Shopmen stood before
their shops calling "Rally up! Rally up! Buy! Buy!" and
the loud and often musical cries of hucksters offered lav-
ender, Shrewsbury cakes, and hot peasecods. Other voices
demanded pots to solder and knives to grind. Suddenly
progress was halted by a rush of bullocks being driven
down the street to the slaughterhouse. Peale's chair was
surrounded by tossing horns and waving tails, and the hot
breath of the cattle was blown into his face. When that ter-
rifying moment was safely past, Charles could take professional pleasure in the handsome coats of arms on the passing carriages and coaches. White coachmen on the boxes
seemed strange to eyes accustomed to seeing dusky slaves
on the driver's seat.

As he saw the endless network of streets and the teeming throngs on every side, Charles marveled that he once

thought Boston a great city or that he once was impressed by hearing that the population of Philadelphia neared the vast total of 25,000. Captain McLachan had informed him that London probably numbered 800,000, and as his chair was halted by a crush of magnificent carriages on fashionable Regent Street, he was ready to believe that at least 600,-000 of London's inhabitants were on the streets around him.

At last Charles arrived at West's door on Castle Street. With the assurance lent by his fine clothes and with Allen's letter of introduction in his left hand, he used his right to lift the great brass knocker on the door. He asked the servant who opened it to announce him as a student from America. In a moment West came dashing down the stairs, his long, white wool painting smock floating behind him, to greet Peale with exuberant cordiality. With his hand under the visitor's elbow, West led him through a series of lofty rooms, the first hung with sketches and cartoons for large paintings; another embellished with sculpture; the last a large painting room with some of his canvases hung on the walls and a partly finished painting on the great easel. Everywhere were detail studies of hands, heads, bits of landscape, or classic architecture.

As West caught sight of the unfinished work on the easel, he exclaimed, "Your hand, Mr. Peale, is just what I need for this figure in the foreground. Pray stand there just a moment until I sketch it in." Peale, in something of a daze, posed, glad of a chance to observe the great artist at work. West was two and a half years older than Peale, a well-built man of medium height, fair, with piercing eyes. He was neatly dressed beneath the painting gown, carefully shod, his hair powdered——

The image wavered. Poor Charles, still feeble from weeks of seasickness, grew faint. West was all apologies, applied restoratives, insisted that Peale rest for a time, and as soon as Charles's color changed to a more wholesome tint, set out with him to find lodgings nearby. On Golden Square at the corner of Silver Street—Peale hoped those names were a good omen—quarters were found, and West briskly bullied the landlady into quoting a fair price. Meanwhile Charles looked out of the window at Golden Square with its neat green lawns crisscrossed by graveled walks and watched workmen who were replacing the wooden fence around it with a handsome iron grille. West pointed out a house on the square that was occupied by Angelica Kauffmann, well known as a painter in a day when women artists were few. Then he insisted upon going with Peale to collect his modest baggage at the inn and saw him installed in his room.

Promising to begin his instruction the next day, West left his pupil to collect his bewildered thoughts. Charles was warm with gratitude for the generous helpfulness of his countryman and vowed he would be worthy of it by making every moment count for the advancement of his painting.

9

Peale Meets Dr. Franklin
and Sees a Mirage Fade Away

PEALE LIVED up to the vow he made to himself that February day in 1767 when he met West by devoting himself heart and soul to his painting under West's instruction. He found West's daily schedule admirable. The artist rose early to plan his compositions before breakfast and then saw his pupils, criticizing their work and giving them instruction until ten. His own painting occupied the hours up to four o'clock, when, changing to formal attire, he received visitors until dinnertime. The evening was devoted to making detail sketches for the big canvases, and Peale found he could be useful in posing for studies of hands or, swathed in classical garments, for the lines of drapery.

His first letter to his friend Bordley reflects his admiration for West:

I have (God be praised) Past through the many dangers of the seas and am now at my studies with Mr West who gives me encouragement to persue my plan of Painting and Promises me all the instruction he is capable of giving. I have seen Reynolds and Cotes who are called the Best Painters and in my humble opinion Mr Wests work Exceeds them all by far. . . . He paints a great deal of History latterly and is excessively fond of it and their is no other eminent in that way at present. . . . Mr West is intimate with the Best Miniature Painter and intends to borrow some Miniature Pieces for me to Coppey privately as he does nothing in that way himself.

"Coppeying" miniatures was in line with West's advice to Peale. Realizing that he needed to make his painting profitable as soon as possible, he advised Charles to perfect himself in the technique of painting on ivory for there was a brisk market for miniatures in England.

So close was Peale's application to his studies that he was practically oblivious to London. It was a glorious period for all the arts. In the literary world the wit and wisdom of Dr. Samuel Johnson were being recorded by an admiring Boswell; David Garrick was the darling of the London stage; Reynolds, Gainsborough, and Romney were immortalizing the beauties and celebrities of the period in their portraits; the dignity of Georgian architecture was in full flower. But Charles barely tasted of this feast; his money must be carefully husbanded and amusements were costly. When he recalled those days years later, he wrote, "Had Mrs Peale accompanied him, he might then have enjoyed the amusements which the great city affords, but he always felt himself lonely even amidst the crowds." He preferred to spend all his time and energy on his work. "For he was not contented with learning to paint in one way but engaged in the whole circle of arts except that of painting in enamel. And also at modeling and casting in Plaster of Paris. He made some essays at Metzotinto scraping. And his application was such that at several times he nearly brought himself into a state of bad health. But with moderate exercise in the open air, the vigor of youth reinstated him."

Where he found time for open air exercise is a mystery. Not content with painting all day, he spent the evening in study, teaching himself French with Boyer's *French-English Dictionary* and reading technical books on art such as *Kirby on Perspective,* books that one day would stand on the shelf at home beside *The Handmaid to the Arts.*

Peale felt that he should see as many masterpieces of European art as possible; he knew he could learn much from them. But it was not easy to do so, for there were no public collections of art at that time. Private collections were in the great mansions of London or in country houses of the wealthy. Permission to see these works of art had to be obtained from the proprietor, which was accomplished through West. Armed with permission, Peale went to a house famed for its fine Italian and Flemish paintings. As he approached the massive door of the mansion, he noted the handsomely wrought, iron link extinguishers beside the entrance, where evening callers could leave their torches, so essential in traveling through the unlighted streets. He raised the great knocker, which fell with a resounding thump, and the door opened as if by magic, revealing a footman in powdered wig and resplendent livery. A second footman stepped forward to take Peale's cloak and three-cornered hat and indicated a third servant, who led him into the first of a series of splendid rooms. Fires were burning in settings of beautifully sculptured marble mantels; the floors were laid with deep-pile carpets from the Orient; tapestries in glowing colors hung upon the mellow wood-paneled walls enriched with gilded carvings forming frames for the paintings he had come to see. Charles stood entranced before a full-length portrait by Van Dyke, studying the clear flesh tones and the brilliant rendering of lace and fabric. Margaret Peale's son appreciated the beauty of textiles, especially when painted with such mastery. A loud "hurrumph" from the waiting footman woke him from his absorption. Evidently he had stayed too long in this room. With a sigh he bestowed the handsome tip which each servant obviously expected and went on to the next room. Inwardly he cursed the system by which a man indicated his wealth by the number of footmen in his employ. He left the mansion sadly, knowing that his meager funds would not permit further visits of this kind, much as he longed to see the art treasures enshrined in the sumptuous dwellings of London.

One day he wrested himself from his painting long enough to call on a well-known American who was in London to represent the interests of Pennsylvania and other colonies, a man who had done much to bring about the repeal of the Stamp Act, Dr. Benjamin Franklin. Peale was learning his way around London now and found no difficulty in reaching 7 Craven Street, the home of Mrs. Stevenson, where Franklin had lodged during his first two visits to England. He was loved as a father by the Stevenson family.

Charles had no letter of introduction but, since his father had known Franklin slightly, hoped he would be welcome as his father's son. The maidservant who admitted him did not announce him; she simply indicated a door down the corridor. Peale walked quietly to the door and beheld a stout man with thinning, unpowdered hair, handsomely dressed in a "blue-green suit with silver buttons," seated with a pretty young lady on his knee. They were too happily absorbed in each other to notice the visitor, so Charles withdrew slightly, made a quick sketch of the scene in his pocket notebook, and returned to the street door. Now slowly and as noisily as possible, he stomped down the corridor to find that decorum reigned.

Franklin received him cordially. "Yes, I remember your father. He was a schoolmaster in Maryland. I met him on one of my tours around the colonies when I was deputy postmaster; he told me much about the London General Post Office where he had been employed."

Charles said, "We are all grateful to you for the improvement you effected in the postal service at home. If my letters reach my wife safely, I have you to thank, sir."

Peale spied a clock on the mantel and spoke of it as only an expert watchmaker could. Franklin told him of a clock he had invented, which showed hours, minutes, and seconds, with a simple mechanism of three wheels and two pinions. With the discovery of a common interest in mechanics, Franklin led the way to his laboratory where he was making experiments in electricity. Charles had heard about Franklin's exploit with a kite in a thunderstorm, by which means he had proved that electricity and lightning were one and the same element. While electricity was somewhat outside Peale's field, he was ready to learn more about this mysterious force, examining Franklin's equipment with fascinated interest. The laboratory was chilly.

Franklin remarked, "If only I had here one of the stoves I invented, we should be more comfortable." He went on to explain the principle of the Franklin stove which was set outside the fireplace, burned less fuel, and threw more heat into a room. Peale, while the doctor talked, observed his kindly expression, the gray eyes alight with intelligence beneath the domed brow, the head large in proportion to the stocky body. He would put all this on canvas one day.

Peale was such a responsive listener that Franklin talked on, jumping from subject to subject. Finally, he spoke of smallpox, the scourge which took such a heavy toll of lives throughout the world, leaving the few survivors hideously scarred. Experiments had been tried in England, following an Oriental practice of implanting virulent matter from the pustules of a victim of the disease under the skin of a well person. If he survived the infection which set in, he seemed to be protected against taking the fever.

Franklin sighed, "I wish I had had the courage to have tried inoculation on my little son. He might not have died of the smallpox."

The clock on the mantel chimed the hour, and Charles realized he was staying far too long. He took his departure, pleased that Dr. Franklin had urged him to call again.

Charles made another visit, this time to present Bordley's letter to his stepfather Edmond Jenings, a contact that resulted in continuing kindness and helpfulness to Peale. Jenings took Peale to the Doctors' Commons where Dr. Charles Wilson's will was recorded, only to find that the property had been left to his surviving daughter and would go to the Peales only if she died without issue. As a prelude to this investigation, Charles had written to an uncle, the Reverend Digby, asking about the Captain Digby who had written Peale at the time of his marriage. Peale showed the reply to Jenings. There had never been a Captain Digby in the family.

"A hoax, my boy," said Jenings. "That letter was a hoax. Can you think of anyone who would have written it to plague you?"

Charles thought back to the time when the letter arrived, just after his term of apprenticeship had ended.

"There was a clever clerk at Nathan Waters's. He always jeered at me when I talked about my inheritance. He must have written the letter."

In the course of the inquiries, a hint that Charles Peale might have had a wife in London before he left for America came to light. At that point his son dropped the investigation and thus happily escaped learning of his father's criminal record. Now the golden mirage would never shine upon the Peales again.

As the first year of Charles's stay in London drew to a close, his funds had dwindled to almost nothing. He wrote to Barrister Carroll that he would come home as soon as the money was gone. Carroll urged him to stay on—the voyage was such a big undertaking that he should make the most of being in London—and authorized his agent to advance him ten guineas. Benjamin West agreed with Carroll and generously took Peale under his own roof to save him the cost of lodgings, giving him, in addition, portrait commissions which he had no time to execute. Charles did all he could to show his gratitude. He posed for West, kept his clocks and watches in order, and mended his favorite palette so skillfully that West never used any other.

Charles made friends with a London jeweler on the

grounds of his interest in watchmaking. The jeweler secured commissions for miniatures for him, profiting himself
by the transaction in making jeweled settings for the
ivories. At first Peale charged two guineas a portrait, raised
the price to three, and then, foolishly, asked four guineas.
At that price the customers could go to a well-known artist,
and Peale's golden goose ceased laying.

Edmond Jenings tactfully aided Peale by giving him
orders to paint members of his family and relatives. The
delicacy of giving help by this means was appreciated by
the proud young artist. Years later he wrote to Jenings,
"When you express pleasure in being my benefactor, I am
glad that I was poor and in want of a friend."

It was well for Peale's future that necessity kept him
at portrait painting. West, whose interest lay in huge
historical compositions, would have liked to see Charles
engage in similar projects. But Peale's gift lay in portraiture, where his penetrating observation and honest realism
found expression. He was not entirely happy in London.
It may have been because he was not able to work as West
did with sincerity, which gave him a feeling of disloyalty
to his teacher.

Peale's work could now rank with that of the best English artists. Three of his miniatures and two oils were hung
in the 1768 exhibition of the Society of Artists, paintings
of two of Bordley's sons among them. When news of that
triumph, long weeks in transit, finally reached Annapolis,
there must have been great rejoicing in the Peale household.

Though Charles by-passed the cultural attractions of
London, he watched political affairs with keen attention

for anything that had a bearing on the American colonies. He was still an American patriot and seethed with indignation when unjust restrictions were imposed on his fellow countrymen. His wrath was aroused by duties levied by the new Chancellor of the Exchequer, Charles Townshend, which affected glass, tea, lead, and painter's colors. The last irked Peale particularly. Because the taxes were light, Townshend did not think the colonists would object to them, but he neglected to consult them on the matter. They promptly threatened boycott of all imported goods and rebelled at the machinery set up for enforcement of the Townshend Act. Commissioners appointed by the crown resided in the colonies but were not subject to local jurisdiction. Armed with writs of assistance, they searched private houses and places of business for smuggled goods.

Peale rejoiced when he heard of the furious resistance of the colonists to the writs of assistance; they were ready to take up arms to protect their private property from search. The assembly of New York refused to quarter the king's troops that were sent to enforce the law. Parliament immediately suspended the New York legislature until it agreed to comply with regulations. That suspension inspired Peale to stage his private revolt against the king. Never, when the royal coach passed in the London streets, would he, as was the custom, doff his hat. Instead he yanked it farther down on his head, a gesture of defiance which gave him a great deal of satisfaction.

Charles marveled at Benjamin West's ability to keep the close friendship and patronage of King George, since he made no effort to conceal his sympathy for the American rebels. He was entirely open in his admiration for their strong resistance to the Stamp Act, which made its repeal inevitable.

As Peale's second year in London neared its end, Edmond Jenings gave him an important commission. Richard Henry Lee, of Virginia, asked Jenings to choose an artist to paint a portrait of the Earl of Camden, a British statesman who consistently opposed the Stamp Act and other methods of taxing the colonies and who was hostile to the present British colonial policies. The portrait was ordered for the Westmoreland County Association which, under the leadership of Lee, had acted powerfully against the Stamp Act. The members wanted a likeness of this friend of the colonies, their hero Camden. Jenings felt that the commission must go to West, but he refused to have that patriotic American, Peale, passed by.

He gave Peale an order to paint another British statesman, beloved by Americans for his advocacy of a conciliatory policy toward the colonists, William Pitt, the Earl of Chatham. He had spoken the words which rang so sweetly in American ears in a session of Parliament called to consider the repeal of the Stamp Act, "I rejoice that America has resisted. Three millions of people so dead to all feelings of liberty as voluntarily to submit to be slaves, would have been fit instruments to make slaves of the rest." He then proposed that the act be repealed. Jenings intended to make Peale's portrait his personal gift to the patriotic gentlemen of Westmoreland County.

Pitt was ill at the time, and it was impossible for Peale to arrange a sitting. He did the best he could, using sculptures of Pitt for models. As Peale built up his composition, the influence of West was evident, for it was a classical allegory. Pitt, dressed in a toga, stands before a Roman altar. One hand holds the Magna Charta, while the other points to a statue of British Freedom trampling upon the rights of New York State as symbolized by the New York coat of arms. The canvas, eight by five feet, is adorned with scrolls, edifices, and such a complicated collection of symbolic objects that an explanatory pamphlet had to be issued as a key.

The style was foreign to Peale, and the result was a mediocre painting. It was, however, enthusiastically received by the Virginians when it arrived accompanied by Jenings's letter to Richard Henry Lee:

> The honest cause of America hath been supported with true liberality by that great man, Lord Chatham. I could wish that his merits were not forgot, and therefore take the liberty of sending you by Captain Johnston his portrait, which, if you think worthy of acceptance of the Gentlemen of Westmoreland, I beg you would offer it in my name. It was executed by Mr Peele of Maryland, who was recommended to me by several friends in that Province, as a young man of merit and modesty. I have found him so and heartily wish he may meet with every encouragement on his return to America, which I believe will be soon, he having made great actual Proficiency and laid grounds, I hope, of perfection in his art.

The Pitt portrait was of such importance to Peale that, before releasing it, he made a somewhat smaller replica to take to America. In 1774 Peale presented the replica to the State of Maryland, and it is displayed today in the State House in Annapolis. Banking on Pitt's popularity in America, Peale also made a large mezzotint plate of the painting; he expected to sell many prints when he reached home. He submitted a proof from the plate to Dr. Franklin, who pronounced it a good likeness of the eminent statesman.

Now, happy thought to homesick Peale, it was time to go home.

10

An Artist
Returns to Maryland

Peale was fortunate again in having free passage offered him. Happy to be going home, he hastily prepared his belongings for shipping. The Pitt portrait was carefully boxed; the huge mezzotint plate was protected by heavy wrappings; bundles of sketches and copies of European paintings, some by West, were crated; and a good stock of painting materials, not obtainable in Annapolis, were securely packed. These tasks were simple; the problem was to prepare for shipment a large revolving platform and a handsome model's chair which West had given Charles from his own studio. But the Son of Liberty refused to take back any clothing except that which was absolutely necessary for the voyage. Much as he was tempted to take gifts to his family, he did not buy any manufactured articles. He showed himself a staunch supporter of nonimportation.

The voyage home was slow, and the weather was pleasant. The sea was so calm that Peale was able to paint a miniature of the captain and oils of two passengers. There was time for reading, and Peale read every one of the thirty-two volumes in the captain's well-selected library. At the end of twelve weeks, on June 8, 1769, Charles Willson Peale set foot on Maryland soil on the shores of the Patuxent River. He chafed at the delays incident to shipping his baggage home by barge, for he was wild with impatience to see his family after two lonely years.

It was late evening when he reached Annapolis unheralded. He had traveled faster than the news of the ship's arrival, and he was only vaguely expected to return sometime during the summer. His heart was beating furiously as he approached his home, and he paused before entering to peer through a window. There they were: Rachel, more beautiful than ever, his serene, handsome mother, and his two brothers. Their heads were bent over a songbook; the sweetly blended voices floated out to him. Good Peggy Durgan sat dozing in her armchair in the corner. But he saw no two-year-old James in the room; perhaps he was asleep. Now he flung open the door and ran into the room. A scene of joyous confusion ensued. Charly clasped Rachel in his arms and tried to include his mother in the embrace. James and St. George beat him jovially about the shoulders, while the dogs raced around them in circles, barking hysterically.

When comparative calm was restored, Charly, his brown hair in wild disorder and his neckerchief awry, cried, "Where is the baby?"

Rachel burst into tears, and Peale needed no words to tell him that his little son was dead. The shadow of sorrow fell upon the happy homecoming.

There was no time to indulge in grief; there was much to be done, and at once. Peale must establish himself and get his painting under way immediately, for his debts were waiting for him. His first concern was to find a house with a large, light room for a painting room and with ample space for the family, which now included recently widowed Margaret Jane. When Peale set out to look for a house, he was surprised at the quiet of the tree-shaded streets of Annapolis. He was amazed to see so few people on the streets, and there was hardly a wheeled vehicle in sight. What could be the matter? Then he laughed; Annapolis was just as it always had been, but he was changed after two years in crowded, noisy London.

A house was found, and at once the painting room proved a magnet to visitors. The platform from West was the center of attraction, for Peale loved to put it through its paces, showing how it could be raised and lowered and wheeled about to catch the changing light. On the platform the wide-armed chair invited the full-skirted ladies to sit for their portraits. Wondering admiration greeted the Pitt portrait when all the symbolism had been pointed out and explained. Sketches adorning the walls were examined with interest. Men gazed boldly and the ladies glanced shyly at a copy, painted by West, of Titian's "Venus," which displayed a fascinating expanse of feminine nudity. The Peale family led a life without privacy, but bore with the inconvenience since sightseeing in the painting room was excellent advertising for Peale and brought in orders for portraits in increasing numbers.

During his brother's absence in London, James had apprenticed himself to a carpenter; now he offered his services as frame maker to the artist. Charly accepted the offer but had something better in mind for talented James.

He taught him all he had learned about miniature painting, with the result that in time James became the better miniaturist of the two and enjoyed a successful career in that field. The two brothers worked together in making a large number of prints from the mezzotint of Pitt. But to Peale's great disappointment, for he had counted on a good income from the prints, relatively few copies were sold.

Annapolis could not furnish Peale with an inexhaustible supply of sitters, but constant demands for portraits from the plantation families suggested that it might be profitable for the artist to go to his patrons. Charly worked out a practicable painting kit which could be carried on horseback. A folding easel, constructed by James, fitted compactly into a leather case; canvas was rolled in such a way that it could be strapped to the back of the saddle; and paints and brushes were neatly packed into the saddlebags. Wearing a brace of handsome pistols, Peale rode first to the nearby plantations; then he traveled farther and farther from home, staying at the homes of his sitters until portraits were finished. His intelligence and charm made him welcome everywhere. He gave his portraits an individual touch by introducing glimpses of a local landscape in the background or by adding objects which suggested the interests or occupation of his subjects. The bits of landscape gave his clients an idea. Would he paint portraits of their estates? This proved a profitable addition to his work, and the small, faithfully represented sketches of mansions and grounds are the prized possessions of many southern families today.

He was to go still farther afield to meet a client. Edmond Jenings had reached out from London to secure for Peale a commission to paint John Dickinson, of Philadelphia, author of "Letters of a Pennsylvania Farmer." Published in 1768, these letters courageously pointed out the peril to the colonists' constitutional rights from recent acts of the British Parliament. Though he was a staunch Loyalist, Dickinson, in his "Letters," implored King George to heal the disputes between Britain and the colonies by peaceful means and avoid the possibility of armed rebellion. He pointed out that wisdom and moderation in settling differences would make the king's name glorious to posterity.

Peale found Dickinson an interesting type to paint. Ashy pale, slender as a reed, he looked as if he might not survive the next month, though he really was tough in fiber and full of vitality. He had a fascinating nose, long and slender like an exclamation point in his intellectual countenance.

In securing the Dickinson commission, Jenings's purpose was to acquaint prominent Philadelphians with Peale's fine portraiture, feeling certain that he would build up an important clientele in that capital and center of colonial life. He was right. John Cadwalader admired the portrait of his cousin Dickinson so much that he asked to be painted next. Other orders followed, several from Marylanders who were now leading merchants in Philadelphia. In addition Peale sold twenty copies of the Pitt engraving, an unexpected windfall.

Dickinson and Cadwalader urged Peale to settle in Philadelphia; there was a good future for him there. But Peale refused to consider it until he had discharged the debts incurred in Maryland. Progress in clearing his indebtedness was slow, for equipping his new home had been costly and he had a large family to maintain. However, he was free to make long stays in Philadelphia each year, in 1770 remaining long enough to justify taking Rachel and their infant daughter Eleanor with him. John Bordley now spent much of his time in Philadelphia, painting a good deal. The two men, always good friends, were drawn closer by this common interest.

Peale wrote a cheerful report on his progress to Dr. Franklin in London, "Since my return the encouragement and patronage I have met with exceed my most sanguine expectation . . . the people here have a growing taste for the arts."

Franklin's reply, dated July 4, 1771, contained practical advice:

If I were to advise you, it should be, by great industry and frugality to secure a competency; for as your profession requires good eyes and cannot so well be followed with spectacles, and therefore, will not afford subsistence for so long a time as other employments, you have a right to claim proportionately large awards. . . . The Arts have always traveled westward and there is no doubt of their flourishing hereafter on our side of the Atlantic.

Peale was thoughtful of his good friends in London. To Jenings he sent a portrait of his stepson Bordley, with American wild flowers in the foreground, flowers that Jenings longed to see. With the portrait Peale sent a parcel of sassafras, which he recommended highly as a medicinal tea. Sketches of Philadelphia went to West to recall the scenes of his childhood, and West returned the compliment by frequent gifts of drawings, prints, and books, among them Pilkington's *Gentleman's and Connoisseur's Dictionary of Painters.* Peale births and deaths were registered in this book rather than in the family Bible. West wrote that Copley was now working with him, for Copley, a Loyalist, had fled from the revolutionary atmosphere of Boston to make London his permanent home. Peale was sorry that Copley had chosen to leave the American colonies when they were struggling to establish the right to govern themselves.

On one of his Philadelphia painting tours, Peale had a commission which resulted in a long, congenial friendship with the sitter, David Rittenhouse, astronomer and man of science. Rittenhouse, a farmer's son, gifted with remarkable mathematical and mechanical ability, had educated himself by reading a collection of technical books left to him by an uncle and scientific works secured for him by a friendly clergyman. He developed great skill in instrument making and, because of his absorption in astronomy, used his skill in improving the efficiency of the telescope. He also constructed an orrery, an instrument which shows the positions and movements of bodies in the solar system. Peale was fascinated by this complicated mechanism, which towered over him in a frame eight feet high. The orrery was divided into three compartments, one showing the celestial system, another the motion of the planets around the earth, and the third the movement of the satellites around the planets. The heavenly bodies were represented by tiny globes of metal, accurately proportioned one to another, which were set in motion by a complex of wheels controlled by a handle at the side of the frame. It was a mystery to Peale how eclipses of the sun and moon, in past and future, could be shown by such means; he thought Rittenhouse might well be proud to have his name and the date 1768 inscribed on the frame. The mechanism of the orrery suggested clockworks, and the artist and the astronomer found they were brother clockmakers and enjoyed some good shoptalk about time-pieces.

During this stay in Philadelphia, Peale met, and gave some lessons to, the "female miniaturist" Polly Wrench. He found her work fairly good but deplored the fact that she limited herself to painting women because it was too embarrassing for a lady to stare fixedly at a man, even in the cause of painting his likeness.

When he returned home, he found that Rachel had been desperately ill with smallpox and, though recovering, still was confined to her darkened room. Peale tortured himself with reproaches. Why had he not tried to protect her against the disease by inoculation? If he had put into practice what Dr. Franklin had told him about such immunization, he might have saved her from disfigurement. He dreaded the day when Rachel would come out into bright light and he would have to see scars on her once smooth and lovely face. But when at last she came out into the sunlight, he saw that by some miracle she had escaped the ugly pockmarks.

Once more death claimed one of Peale's children, a baby girl called Margaret Bordley, leaving Eleanor the sole survivor of the four children born to them. When little Margaret was laid out for burial, she looked so exquisitely beautiful that Peale felt he must preserve that beauty in a painting. While he was working, Rachel came to sit beside the little one, tragic in her grief, and the artist with rapid strokes included her in the composition. Rachel could never bear to look at that vivid reminder of her sorrow and covered it with a curtain when Peale hung it in the painting room. At times the curtain was drawn aside for visitors to Peale's studio in Philadelphia such as John Adams, delegate to Congress from Massachusetts.

Adams wrote to his wife Abigail:

Yesterday I took a walk into Arch Street to see Mr Peale's painting room. Peale is from Maryland, a tender, soft, affectionate creature. . . . He showed me a moving picture. His wife all bathed in tears with a child about six months laid out in her lap. The picture struck me prodigiously. . . . Peale is ingenious. He has vanity, loves finery, speaks French, is capable of friendship and strong family attachments and natural affections.

The "tender, soft, affectionate creature" later painted an excellent portrait of Mr. Adams.

Among new friends in Annapolis was Reverend Jonathan Boucher, who admired Peale both as an artist and as a man. In 1772 Boucher was tutoring an unruly lad from Virginia, John Parke Custis, stepson of Colonel George Washington. Peale had never met Washington, though he came to Annapolis frequently for the races and the theater. Now Reverend Boucher was to be instrumental in getting a commission for Peale, which was of importance to the painter but of far greater importance to succeeding generations of Americans.

11

Peale Paints
Colonel Washington

COLONEL GEORGE WASHINGTON was being besieged in his
Virginia home, Mount Vernon on the Potomac River, an
estate he had inherited in 1763. The light and heavy artillery of feminine persuasion had been brought to bear on
him, and he was at the point of capitulation to a charming
one-woman army.

More than ten years ago, after playing an important part
in the British campaign which ended the long French and
Indian War, Washington had come to Mount Vernon to
exchange military life for the peaceful occupation of
gentleman-farmer. For the past few years he had varied his
rural existence with sessions at Williamsburg as a member
of the Virginia House of Burgesses. None of the fiery eloquence he had heard at those stormy sessions could have
been more effective than that of his energetic little wife
Martha, formerly the widow Custis, as she insisted that he
have "his likeness limned." The brave soldier was forced
to surrender, but he did so at his own terms, "Very well,

Madam, but only if you and your children have your likenesses taken at the same time."

Not knowing any artists, the Washingtons asked Reverend Boucher, Jacky Custis's tutor in Annapolis, to suggest
someone. Boucher said he knew the very man for them.
Charles Willson Peale was the finest artist in the field and
in addition, a charming, cultivated person whose acquaintance would be agreeable to them.

Peale promptly received an invitation to come to Mount
Vernon to paint an oil portrait of Colonel Washington and
miniatures of Mrs. Washington and Jacky and Patty Custis.
He looked forward to meeting this Virginia gentleman who
was famous as a military man of great ability and as an
American patriot.

Boucher warned Charles that the Washingtons lived
with considerable formality and that he should equip himself with a suitable wardrobe. Peale chose his apparel carefully, packed a good supply of fresh linen, and with his
painting kit in good order started off on the ride to Mount
Vernon with Jacky Custis. Jacky was a lively lad—too
lively, his tutor thought—but he proved to be an amusing traveling companion and the ride southward passed
quickly. Peale noted that the roads were somewhat improved now that stagecoaches were making regular runs
between the towns.

Peale's breath was taken away by his first glimpse of
Mount Vernon. The white-pillared house, set on a hill
sloping to the river which half-circled its foot in a wide
loop, was surrounded by velvety lawns and fine trees clad
in the delicate green of May. As they rode closer, gardens
and orchards and the many small buildings which were

clustered about the mansion came into view. At the sound
of hoofbeats, Negro grooms rushed from the stables to
take the horses and a plump little woman with brown hair
and sparkling hazel eyes ran out of the house to clasp
Jacky in her motherly arms. Mrs. Washington warmly welcomed Peale and presented him to the frail dark girl
who had come out to the portico, her daughter Patty Custis.

"Colonel Washington will be here in a short while, Mr.
Peale," said Mrs. Washington. "Let Jody take you to your
room, where you can refresh yourself and remove the dust
of travel."

Charles followed the smiling slave up the graceful stair-
way to a bedroom. From its dormer windows he admired
the magnificent view of the winding Potomac.

When Peale came down, in a dark red coat and pale-
gray breeches, neatly gartered white stockings and silver-
buckled shoes, his hair in a trim queue, Washington was
awaiting him. Charles was impressed by the colonel's physical appearance; he was six feet two inches tall and had a
lean, large-boned frame. The artist's fingers itched to begin putting on canvas the rugged face with steel-blue eyes,
strong nose, and wide, generous mouth. After dinner he
was further impressed by Washington's muscular strength
when the male guests amused themselves by throwing a
heavy metal bar in a contest to see who could toss it
farthest. The colonel picked it up easily and threw it far
beyond any mark which had been made.

The portrait got under way at once but without much
cooperation from the sitter, according to Washington's
own description:

I am now, contrary to all expectations, under the hands of Mr Peale, but in so grave, so sullen a mood, and now and then under the influence of Morpheus when some critical strokes are making, that I fancy the skill of this gentleman's pencil will be put to it in describing what manner of man I am.

The "gentleman's pencil" (which meant brush in those days) did very well, showing Washington as a colonel of the Virginia militia in a uniform of blue coat with red facings and red breeches. The portrait called to mind the young man who, having exchanged his surveyor's instruments for an officer's uniform, led a motley crew of woodsmen and friendly Indians to battle with the French and their savage allies. The painting is the only likeness of the young Washington, and thanks to Peale's straightforward realism, it has preserved a true picture of the man.

Work on the portrait progressed rapidly, according to Washington's diary:

May 18 (1772). Mr Peale came to Mount Vernon.
May 20. Set to have my portrait drawn.
May 21. I set again to take the drapery.
May 22. Set to Mr Peale to finish my face. In afternoon rid with him to my mill.

Peale stayed on to do miniatures of Martha Washington and John Custis. He worked when he could on an ivory of Patty Custis, an invalid not strong enough to pose long at a time. Meanwhile he enjoyed the life at Mount Vernon. Guests constantly arrived by private river barge or on horseback—there seemed no limit to the accommodations for guests in the mansion—and stayed for days or weeks at will. Afternoons the masculine visitors vied with each other in sports or rode with Washington, who was a superb horseman. In the evening the guests would take a stroll about the grounds and later join in dancing, which was considered properly mild exercise for delicate Patty. Washington was fond of "stepping to a tune," especially when the tune was played on the spinet by his adored wife. Nowadays his wife was not dressed in silks and satins, for she heartily supported the boycott of importations from Britain. In fact, she had organized a group of spinners and weavers who, using raw materials grown on the plantation, made textiles of cotton, wool, and linen to clothe the household. In former years Washington had ordered the loveliest gowns obtainable from England for the adornment of his pretty wife, but now he thought she looked even more handsome in her patriotic garb of homespun.

Mrs. Washington asked her guests to observe a daily routine. At eleven o'clock they all assembled in the drawing room for conversation; at twelve the hostess disappeared, reappearing at precisely one with a slave carrying a huge punch bowl filled with a delicious, potent beverage. Youthful spies, curious to know what Mrs. Washington did in that absent hour, hid under her bed and discovered that she spent the time mixing the punch in her room, not trusting it to any other hand.

When the four portraits were finished, they met with enthusiastic approval. For twenty-seven years the portrait of Washington was a cherished ornament of Mount Vernon; it is now the property of Washington and Lee University. Washington wore the miniature of Martha to the day of his death, and the miniature of Patty became doubly precious after her death a year later. The colonel's account book shows the prices paid for the portraits:

May 30. Pay Mr Peale for drawing my picture   £18.4.0
      Miniature for Mrs Washington   13.0.0
      "   " Miss Custis   13.0.0
      "   " Mr Custis   13.0.0
                                  £57.4.0

The sullen mood in which Washington claimed to have begun his sittings with Peale was soon dissipated, for he took a great liking for the artist, which persisted over many years and survived sitting for fourteen original portraits. Without these records the appearance of Washington in the Revolutionary period would be little known. It is believed that Peale's likenesses are more faithful than the idealized portraits that were painted after Washington became a national hero. This belief is based on the evidence of a life mask made in 1783 by Joseph Wright, one of West's pupils, who was sent to America to make the mask for use in the construction of an equestrian statue of Washington in London. Washington vividly describes this ordeal:

Wright oiled my features and placing me on my back on a cot, proceeded to daub my face with plaster. Mrs Washington entered the room and seeing my face overspread with plaster, cried out. Her cry excited in me a disposition to smile which gives my mouth a slight twist or compression of the lips, now observable in the bust which Wright afterward made.

Despite that slight accident, the mask can be used as a measure of the accuracy of other likenesses of Washington, and by that test Peale's portraits are by all odds the most like the original. He cared too much for realism to idealize the small eyes or modify the ruggedness of the face.

But this is all in the future. For the present there exists

only that first portrait of Colonel Washington, hardly dry, from the brush of Charles Willson Peale.

Before Peale left Mount Vernon, Colonel Washington, enthusiastic about his outstanding skill as a painter and captivated by the man's wide range of interests and attractive personality, made a recommendation which proved useful to Peale. He urged him to make a long detour to Williamsburg on his way home to try it out as a field for commissions. He wrote letters of introduction to important persons in Williamsburg, commending him highly as a portraitist. Peale gladly followed this suggestion and had a rewarding sojourn in that lovely town, making the acquaintance of Virginians whom he would encounter again in later years. A letter to Mr. Thomas Jefferson, member of the House of Burgesses, was not presented, for that gentleman had just married and did not go to Williamsburg that year. But Peale met him on a subsequent visit.

Weary but elated with the success of the early summer of 1772, Peale returned to Annapolis. From there he wrote his sympathetic friend Bordley, "My reputation is greatly increased by a Number of New Yorkers haveing been here who have given me the character of being the best painter of America—that I paint more certain and handsomer Likenesses than Copley." To the man who had been a green beginner when Copley was an arrived artist, this praise was sweet.

Indeed his work had reached a high point; he achieved excellent likenesses, his color had warmth, and the arrangement of his compositions was outstandingly good. Peale could lend vivacity to the expression of his subjects and had the ability to portray character with depth and reality. He had learned to use the materials of his craft with great care, preparing his canvases both front and back to make them strong and enduring. He was also successful in achieving flesh tones which did not darken with time, a fault of his earlier work which caused him much distress. Tones in his color had delicacy and lightness, lending his paintings a lyrical grace. Peale tried by every means to attain reality in his portraits, at one time experimenting with brushes four feet long with the idea that he could better compare the canvas with the sitter at that distance. Whatever his technical methods, he had reached his full stature as an artist of skill and distinction. He was ready for the demands which would now be put upon him.

12

Peale Rides Off
in All Directions

FOR THE NEXT few years, 1772–1775, Peale was constantly on the move as demands for portraits came from tidewater Virginia and Maryland, Philadelphia, Baltimore, and Williamsburg. He made it a point, however, always to be in Annapolis for the racing season, not so much because he loved the sport, but because it gave him the opportunity to come in contact with the world of fashion, the source of his best clientele. Poor Rachel had to be content with bits and pieces of her Charly's time, but she was glad of his popularity and grateful for the prosperity it brought. The debts were being paid gradually. That was worth any sacrifice.

At times it was difficult to collect payment for the portraits. In September, 1774, Peale put a notice in the *Maryland Gazette*, "If a certain E.V. does not immediately pay for his family picture, his name shall be published full length in the next paper." Next week the *Gazette* announced, "Mr Elie Valette, pay me for painting your family picture, Charles Peale." Mr. Valette came back at Mr.

Peale in the following issue, "Yes, you shall be paid, but not before you learn to be less insolent."

While the roads were deep in mud and winter weather made travel well-nigh impossible, Peale felt he could spare some time for a project dear to his heart—a large painting of the entire family. He shows them sitting around a table—Mrs. Peale at one end with little Eleanor on her lap, Elizabeth next to her, and Peggy Durgan standing just behind, her arms folded; St. George is at the other end of the table, sketching his mother, while James, Charles, and Margaret Jane look on; Rachel is seated in the center holding the baby Raphaelle. In the background, above their heads, are three busts marked B. West, C. W. Peale, and E. Jenings. A classical sketch appears on an easel in back of Charles. Years later Peale added a faithful family dog to the foreground. When John Adams saw the painting in Philadelphia, he wrote Abigail, "There is a happy cheerfulness in their countenances and a familiarity in their air toward each other." Peale indeed captured the loving solidarity of that congenial group of handsome people and caught for posterity, in perhaps the most charming group painting in early American art, an exceptionally fine family relationship.

In the winter of 1774 Peale had the promise of so much work in Baltimore that he established himself there with Rachel and Eleanor for several months. They had comfortable quarters, including a large painting room for Peale, on the second floor of a wholesale shop on Market Street. Rachel was homesick for Annapolis, but she amused herself by exploring the muddy streets of Baltimore. As a housekeeper she admired the convenience of the town's water system. A large basin on a hill, filled by water pumped from springs, supplied various parts of the town with pure water, thanks to lead pipes and the power of gravity. Much better, Rachel thought, than drawing it out of a well. She often walked past three public institutions. One was a home for unmarried men, who were housed, fed, and permitted to carry on their trades; the second was for spinsters, a hive of chattering women engaged in embroidery and weaving. Rachel thought the girls looked pale and languid because of the overefficient Dutch stoves in the workrooms. Widows lived in the third establishment, which had an adjoining chapel. The chapel was interesting to the artist's wife because of the paintings with which the widows had adorned the walls. John Adams inspected these paintings, too, and reported that they were "done with strong colors and very violent passions, but not in very good taste."

Evenings in their Baltimore home were lively and pleasant, thanks to James Alcock, who was an excellent French scholar. Formerly a London merchant, he now conducted an elementary school. Charles recalled in his memoirs:

Peale engages him to teach himself, wife and Pupil in evenings in Peale's rooms. The day being occupied with setters and their company, the time of candlelight was welcome when this little company resumes their amusements of comment-vous portez-vous. . . . A rule was made that whoever should speak one word of English must pay a forfeit . . . the amount to furnish cakes for the company.

Once again Peale was painting patriotic banners. The Independent Company of Baltimore ordered one, and Peale painted "Liberty Beside the Sea" with the legend "Representation or No Taxation." Wherever he went, Peale kept closely in touch with patriot activities, giving what aid he could to the cause of American freedom.

Homecoming from Baltimore was joyous indeed. The happiness of the family reunion was exceeded by the relief of being able at last to pay his debts; the stay in Baltimore had been truly profitable. Peale exclaimed fervently, "Thank God! I have nothing but debts of gratitude."

Peale took part with the Sons of Liberty in an Annapolis "tea party" nearly a year after Boston had dumped thousands of pounds' worth of tea in its harbor in protest against the British Tea Act. The act allowed the East India Company to bring tea in its own ships directly to dealers in the colonies, enabling them to undersell those dealers who had to pay heavy import duties on stock from England or Holland. Philadelphia and New York had not allowed the tea ships to land, and Charleston, in South Carolina, had impounded a cargo and refused to allow its sale. An Annapolis shipowner, Anthony Stewart, had allowed the East India Company to use his brig *Peggy Stewart* to bring a ton of tea to Annapolis. The ship could not land until the duty was paid on the tea. In the interests of the passengers (or so he said), Stewart paid the tax on the cargo. Immediately the patriot citizens of Annapolis rose in protest; the Sons of Liberty erected a gallows in front of Stewart's house and an angry mob threatened to destroy the house, which was far more valuable than a ton of tea. Charles Carroll advised Stewart to burn both ship and cargo. Stewart, vowing that he was a patriot at heart and willing to prove it, placed a committee on board to witness that he carried out orders and beached the *Peggy* on Windmill Point. Fires were set throughout the vessel, and the committee hurriedly scrambled ashore. On shore a great crowd watched the burning ship, faces reddened by the baleful light of the fire. Charles and St. George watched with the rest. When the excitement died down, they walked home slowly, wondering whether Britain would heed protests such as these and modify the unjust Tea Act.

In Annapolis the only tea available, a small supply smuggled from Holland, was strictly rationed. Brief entries in Peale's diary record such rationing along with his daily activities:

October, 1775. Asked permission from Mr Paca to get some tea for Mother who was ill.

Oct. 17. Worked on Miss Key's miniature. Lent Mr Fitzhugh my hunting shirt, mended the string of Mr Rock's Clock.

Oct. 18. Finished Miss Key's head got a note from Mr Paca of leave for W. Hide to sell my mother what tea she might really want.

Oct. 22. Sunday Set up last night with my mother. We were much alarmed by her having a fainting fit. A sermon was preached in town on the times by a traveling preacher to the great satisfaction of the Congregation, recommending spirited measure to fight to the last for Liberty.

Oct. 23. I am obliged to stay with my mother during her taking a puke. Cleaned Mr Pitt's picture and began a coulering to make the face somewhat younger.

Peale was probably putting final touches on the copy of his Pitt portrait before presenting it to the State of Maryland. The assembly accepted it by vote and agreed to offer the artist "as a compliment for his very Genteel present, one hundred pounds Common money." The painting still hangs in the State House in Annapolis.

Once again Rachel and Charly had to bear the loss of a child; this time gay, pretty Eleanor. However, there was the baby boy to console them. They had named him Raphaelle because Pilkington spoke highly in his *Dictionary of Painters* of an Italian painter by that name.

With his debts paid, Peale could now honorably leave Annapolis for the wider opportunities of Philadelphia. It was a big undertaking to transplant the entire family; only St. George would remain in Annapolis. Household goods, including the revolving platform and the model's chair, were sent by barge to the head of Chesapeake Bay, there to await orders for shipment to Philadelphia. On November 2, 1775, Peale put Rachel, Raphaelle, Mrs. Peale, and Peggy Durgan aboard a packet bound for Charlestown on the upper Eastern Shore of the bay. Margaret Jane, who had recently married Nathaniel Ramsay, a lawyer of Charlestown, offered the upper half of her new home to her mother and sister-in-law until Peale could settle them in Philadelphia.

Peale's departure from Annapolis was far from placid. Just as he was ready to start off, his horse Belisarius ran away. Before he could recover the horse, his landlord, Nick McCubbin, seized his four-wheeled traveling sulky for unpaid rent. Peale had given him an order on Barrister Carroll for ten pounds to pay the rent, but McCubbin refused to honor it. Peale gave the money to the sheriff and regained possession of the sulky. Belisarius was captured and harnessed to it, a full painting kit was packed under the seat, and Peale drove down to the Rock Hall ferry which would take him to the Eastern Shore. Belisarius did not care for the ship; he had to be double-tied to keep him from plunging overboard. Safely ashore, Charles drove to his childhood home, Chestertown, where he stopped long enough to paint a miniature. While there he offered his sulky to two young ladies for the drive to their plantation home. As they were riding pleasantly along, a pin which held the two parts of the sulky together gave way. Off went Belisarius with the front wheels, tail in air, neighing shrilly. The passengers were thrown into the roadside herbage, unhurt but making the most of this golden opportunity for violent hysterics. A passing carriage took the tear-stained, rumpled young ladies to their home while Peale gathered up the scattered pieces of his sulky. He borrowed a horse to track down the exuberant Belisarius, who, when found, was securely locked into the stable for a cooling-off period.

With the sulky once more united in all its parts, Peale progressed slowly toward Charlestown, filling a series of portrait commissions. As usual he stayed at his patrons' homes and relieved the strain of painting by practicing marksmanship with the men of the household. Every patriot felt it his duty to become adept in the use of rifle or musket.

The call to arms had been proclaimed; and everywhere local militia were drilling, for war had begun. In the spring the first shots had been exchanged between British regulars and American militia at Lexington, Massachusetts. The Battle of Bunker Hill followed in June, when the rebel soldiers surprised the redcoats by their courage, repulsing the British twice and losing to a bayonet charge only when their powder was gone.

With all his commissions fulfilled, Peale finally drove into Charlestown behind a well-behaved Belisarius to spend several busy, happy weeks with his family. Dressed for work in fringed hunting shirt of deerskin, he ground a good supply of colors in oil, tying them up in bladders of skin to keep them moist, mended the harness for his sulky, put Margaret Jane's watch in order, and assisted Nathaniel Ramsay in making gunpowder. Ramsay had been appointed by his fellow citizens to work on the problem of "cooking" saltpeter out of niter-bearing earth, and Peale lent his inventive mind to the experiments, suggesting ingenious methods for getting results.

It was December 18, 1775, when Peale finally reached Philadelphia. He hastened to see his friend Bordley and found him red-faced and tearful, cooking saltpeter and stirring it with the handle of a frying pan. They exchanged their formulas for gunpowder and called in David Rittenhouse who had produced a formula of his own. The recipe Peale contributed was: "Put peter in water to dissolve it, then mix the cole (charcoal) and sulphur first made fine, stirring well, gently boiling water away till it becomes paste, then pound it." Preparations for war were being made everywhere; it was of the utmost importance for the colonies quickly to manufacture munitions.

In spite of his passionate interest in patriotic pursuits, Peale had to devote himself to a vital personal problem. He must establish himself as a painter in Philadelphia and prepare to settle his family in the national capital.

13

Peale Moves
to Philadelphia

IT WAS MOST difficult to find a house that offered a large
room with proper light for a painting room and also accommodations for the Peale family. He had to count them
over to make sure he had them all in mind. There were his
mother, Rachel, Raphaelle, a new baby named Angelica
Kauffmann in honor of his artist neighbor on Golden Square,
Peggy Durgan, and three slaves. Charlie and Betsey Polk
were taken under the family wing since their father, Elizabeth's husband, was killed in naval action.

While he searched for a house, Charles lived in Mrs.
Yard's boardinghouse, one of several establishments popular with delegates to Congress, most of whom had left their
families at home. They were agreeable places to live in, for
the landladies vied with each other in the excellence of
their table and the level of conversation maintained during
meals by their distinguished paying guests.

Ready to notify Philadelphia that it had an artist of reputation in its midst, he hired boys to distribute handbills to
the homes of the more prosperous citizens, announcing:

Mr Charles Peale presents his compliments to the Ladies and Gentlemen of Philadelphia and begs leave to offer his services to Paint their Portraits in miniature or large, if most agreeable, at their own houses. Mr Peale is to be spoke with at Mrs Yard's, Second Street.

Philadelphia responded to the notice in a most gratifying manner; Peale was kept fully occupied. As he trotted from one house to another to meet his appointments with sitters, he ardently longed for the time when he would have a painting room once more. Passing the State House one day, he met tall, red-haired Thomas Jefferson, now delegate to Congress from Virginia. Both were delighted to renew the slight acquaintance made at Williamsburg on one of Peale's painting tours. They agreed to meet soon for a music session, for Jefferson played the violin. Mr. Jefferson said that he disliked being so far away from his Virginia farm but that he was deeply interested in his work in the Congress. Though Congress still hoped to avoid a complete break with Britain, it had appointed George Washington to command the Continental forces now before Boston. Peale approved the appointment heartily, for he had great faith in the ability and patriotism of his recent patron.

Another friend in Congress—William Paca, of Maryland, who had helped him get tea for his mother in Annapolis— asked Peale if he would let him borrow some miniatures to show John Hancock, president of Congress. If Hancock liked them and ordered a portrait, other delegates, especially those from colonies where there were no artists, would follow suit. Peale thought it an excellent idea and lent Paca several recently completed miniatures.

The samples pleased Mr. Hancock, and he asked Peale to

paint ivories of himself and his wife. The commission delighted Peale, not only because it was a feather in his artist's
cap to paint the president of Congress but because Hancock made a subject of great elegance. Massachusetts-born
Hancock had inherited a large fortune. He set Philadelphia
agog with the splendor in which he rode through the
streets in a sumptuous carriage, attended by four liveried
servants with an escort of fifty horsemen. When Peale went
to the luxurious mansion which the Hancocks had rented,
he found his subject a slender, nervous, foppishly dressed
man. However, Peale was not deceived by the dandified
appearance; he knew there was no lack of manly strength
in this man who ruled Congress justly and with a firm hand.

Mrs. Dorothy Quincy Hancock won Peale's admiration
by her dignity and good breeding. She had been praised by
John Adams because "in large and mixed companies she
is totally silent as a lady ought to be." Alone with Peale, she
chatted about the trouble Mr. Hancock was having with
his watch and confided that one of the servants was constantly tardy because his watch was out of order. Peale with
a customary good nature repaired both timepieces.

The Hancock miniatures brought twelve guineas each,
a better price than London artists received, Peale recalled
with satisfaction.

Peale was still leading a bachelor's existence at Christ-
mastime. However, Christmas Eve was unexpectedly pleasant; he spent it with Dr. Franklin, who was now a congressional delegate. Franklin had grown stouter and gray hair
straggled thinner on the noble dome of his head, but he was
genial and companionable as always. He showed Peale his
recent invention which he called an "Armonica." It con-

sisted of musical glasses, graduated in size, set on a row of iron spindles in a long box. When a handle at the side was turned, the glasses were set spinning. Rubbing the edges of the glasses with moistened fingers produced celestial tones. Charles quickly learned to play it and was not surprised when it became a popular musical instrument.

Dining out occasionally, Peale did not always enjoy the hospitality offered, as the entry in his diary for December 30, 1775, testifies:

Dined with Mr Brooks in company of Methodis Preacher who with all his Sanctity wanted good manners. The Turkey was tuf, the Beef very little better, Jam sour, we had very little charity for the mistress of the entertainment.

Busy as he was in executing portrait commissions, Charles found time to join David Rittenhouse in working on "a Riffle with a telescope to it." It was evidently an attempt to equip a gun with a telescopic sight. The contraption kicked back to administer a fine black eye until they devised a spring to ease the action.

Rittenhouse had been appointed engineer for the Committee of Safety, a body organized to prepare for the defense of the city. Lead was badly needed for bullets, and David was proud of his scheme for securing that essential metal. Going from house to house, he asked the owners to contribute the lead weights from their clocks to the cause and offered iron replacements. A good supply of lead was his reward.

David and Charles constructed a gun with a hollow stock to hold bullets, a wiper, and a ramrod and with a sheath at the side for a bayonet. It was a handy way to keep those articles in one place and immediately at hand.

Patriot activities were quickened in January, 1776, by the publication of Thomas Paine's pamphlet "Common Sense." Franklin had known Paine in London and had persuaded him to emigrate to America. In Philadelphia he had found employment as editor of a magazine. Peale, having met him at Franklin's house after the doctor's return, read his pamphlet. His feelings were stirred as were those of patriots everywhere, for the sale of "Common Sense" was enormous. Paine's demand for the independence of the colonies stiffened the convictions of the rebellious patriots. He advanced convincing reasons for separation from Britain, and his rallying cry, "Ye that dare oppose not only the tyranny but the tyrant stand forth!" touched a responsive chord in thousands of hearts.

Peale had not yet found a house, partly because his time was so filled by painting commissions that he could not search for one. A gratifying commission came from a wealthy financier, Robert Morris, who wished to be painted with his wife. Morris had an important countinghouse and carried on an extensive import business, which naturally made him cool to the patriots' boycott of imported goods. Though Peale differed with him on that point, he did not feel that he needed to refuse to paint his portrait. He admired the Morris house, a handsome brick structure with large, many-paned windows and tall dormers. He also appreciated the beauty of the interior, especially the fine mahogany doors with highly polished, skillfully wrought brass fittings.

Arranging Mrs. Morris in the composition was a problem, for her hair was arranged according to the highest fashion. It was literally the highest, for her powdered tresses were arranged over a wire structure fully two feet in height, with adornments of plumes, flowers, and ribbon bows. As Peale painted the headdress, he smiled inwardly, thinking of a story he had heard about a woman of fashion who awoke in terror one night to find that a mouse had invaded her lofty coiffure.

Robert and Mrs. Morris liked Peale so well that they asked him to take tea with them after one of the sittings. The contraband beverage was served in exquisite, tiny porcelain cups, and Charles was glad that he knew what to do when he had finished his twelfth thimbleful. He laid his spoon across the cup, which signified that he would take no more.

There were many lonely evenings for Charles, which he made bearable by constructing a guitar. It was a far better instrument than the fiddle he made aboard the *Brandon*. When it was finished, he strummed accompaniments while singing French love songs to his distant Rachel. Music meant much to Peale; it was almost as essential as food in his daily life.

One day in March, 1776, Peale was walking along Chestnut Street on his way to finish a portrait when he heard the sharp hoofbeats of a hard-ridden horse echoing down the street. Then horse and rider passed in a flash. "Dispatch rider," said Peale to himself as he ran to the Coach and Horse Inn, where the rider had pulled up. Fellow citizens came running from all directions to hear the news; it was good news, which for five days had been relayed from one

rider to another. Washington had forced the British to
evacuate Boston; General Howe with eight thousand troops
and a thousand Boston Loyalists who were afraid to face
returning patriots had sailed for Halifax; the Continental
Army had captured vital stores; after reorganization the
rebel troops would move to New York where Washington
expected the next British attack. Great was the jubilation
among the Philadelphia patriots, but the Loyalists wore
sour faces. Peale learned something of interest to a man
who had painted a good many banners: the Continental
Army was marching under a new flag, thirteen alternating
red and white stripes with the British Union Jack in the
upper corner. The stripes symbolized the thirteen colonies standing together to gain the right to govern themselves.

By spring Peale had enough orders for portraits in
Charlestown to justify spending some weeks with his
family. He made the acquaintance of his daughter Angelica, as pretty as a blond angel in his fond fatherly eyes.
While in Charlestown he experimented with molding
glass to fit over the curved ivory of his miniatures. Glass
was on the nonimportation list, and colonists were learning
to make what they needed. Out of fragments of ivory
Charly carved a few teeth to replace some which Margaret
Jane had lost; he hated to see the gaps in her lovely smile.
They did not last long, but the experiment was worth
trying.

In May a house which met his needs became available
in Philadelpha, a plain brick house on Arch Street, so called
because an arched viaduct carried it over Mulberry Street.
The house was not far from the Delaware River, convenient

to the food markets for which Philadelphia was famous, and only a short distance from the center of town. Orders were given to have the household goods shipped from the head of Chesapeake Bay, and Peale prepared to fetch his family. But a commission of importance delayed all plans.

14

A Bell Is Rung

ON MAY 19, 1775, Peale noted in his diary, "Mr Hancock bespoke a Portrait of Genl. Washington and his Lady."

The general was coming to Philadelphia for a brief consultation with Congress before he left to take up command of the army in New York. There was nothing to do but delay the family move until he had finished this flattering commission. He was soon at work. "May 25, Began ½ length of Mrs Washington. May 29, Began painting Genl. Washington." However, since Washington was pressed for time, Peale had to wait until later in the year to finish the portrait.

Now he was free to arrange for the transportation of his family. Two stage wagons were hired to carry the family and the small baggage. Margaret Jane was coming with them, for her husband, an officer in the Maryland militia, had been called to active service. The move was made on a radiant June day, and the gently rolling countryside, through which the caravan slowly made its way, was richly green with unripe wheat and deep grass. Meadow larks rose from the fields with bursts of lovely song, but not even Peale's sensitive ears could hear them. The springless vehicles moved with a thunderous rumble, wheels squawked, the draft horses plodded along with heavy hoof-beats, and the tired children wailed fretfully.

Lucy, one of the slaves, who was riding in the first wagon to help Rachel with the children, asked permission to take a walk. When the second wagon came along—it had kept far behind to escape the dust raised by the first—the occupants were shocked to find an intoxicated Lucy lying on the side of the road. She was dragged to her feet, doused liberally with cold water, and forced to stumble along beside the wagon to sober up. She was overcome with shame by the time the fumes of alcohol had disappeared. Her conscience had sufficiently punished her, Peale thought, when he finally discovered what had happened. He was a kind master; his slaves were never beaten.

Rachel and Mrs. Peale, impatient to see their new home, pestered Charly with questions as they entered the city. "Is it on this street? Is that the house, Charly?" they asked until they finally came to the plain, square brick house he had rented. The ladies, accustomed to the more graceful outlines of Maryland dwellings, were disappointed. But the comfortable interior pleased them, and they were happy to find that trees in front of the house and in the rear garden kept the house cool on the hottest days. The big painting room was put in order immediately; the familiar furniture from Annapolis was installed, and art books arranged on a shelf and plaster casts of classic sculpture displayed. The family-group painting was hung on the wall with the veiled portrait of Rachel and the dead baby and the ever-popular copy of Titian's "Venus." Prints and Italian drawings sent by West were tastefully hung as were some of Peale's sketches of country houses and estates.

Rachel and Mrs. Peale became homesick for the leisurely life of Annapolis. Philadelphia was all hustle and bustle— thirty thousand people living in one town! In the warm weather the Philadelphians practically lived in the streets. Housewives sat on benches beside their well-scrubbed, snow-white doorsteps, gossiping and exchanging recipes; children played their games with joyful noise; cats, dogs, and chickens were everywhere. On hot days women wore wide, flat hats called "skimmers" to shade their faces; they sometimes protected their complexions with masks held in place by a bar gripped in their teeth. Rachel determined to get a mask, for her skin had been sensitive since the smallpox.

The Peale women felt more at home when they had chosen a church for regular attendance. They selected Christ Church, a Church of England parish, which was near their home on Arch Street. Their musical ears had been pleased by the mellow tones of the eight bells which hung in the steeple. The chimes rang the quarters, halves, and hours during the day, but on Tuesday and Friday evenings such merry tunes were played that people came from miles around to hear them.

The Loyalist members of the Christ Church congregation did not wear homespun. They dressed in silks and velvets and rode to service in chairs or coaches. It was the gayest and most aristocratic congregation in the city. Imagine the chagrin of Mrs. Peale and Rachel one Sunday when their Charly hissed the minister loudly for praying for the English king! The kneeling congregation craned necks to discover where the hisses came from, and the violent blushes of his companions gave the patriot away.

Peggy Durgan had a request to make of Peale. Would he buy her a spinning wheel? She had seen the Committee of Safety establishment at Ninth and Market Streets where volunteers were spinning and weaving the flax, hemp, and wool brought in by the farmers. Peggy wished to do her share at home, and the soothing whir of the wheel was heard as Peggy sat spinning with her eyes on Raphaelle at play and the baby in her cradle. Like other nonimportationists, the Peales ate no lamb. The lambs must be allowed to grow up into wool producers to help the colonists become independent of British textiles.

The Peales often strolled past the State House, a two-storied brick building with a graceful white tower surmounted by a cupola. A bronze bell hung in the tower where it could be seen from the street. Charles showed his family a platform in the State House yard at the rear. From that structure his friend David Rittenhouse, in 1767, had observed the transit of the planet Venus across the sun.

The Third Continental Congress was meeting in the State House, and all Philadelphia knew that important matters were being discussed. On June 7, 1776, Richard Henry Lee, of Virginia, had risen to introduce this resolution:

That the United Colonies are, and by right ought to be, free and independent; that they are absolved from all allegiance to the British Crown; that all political connection between them and the State of Great Britain is, and ought to be dissolved.

The bold words made Peale's heart leap. He was proud of the important roles his friends were playing; Thomas Jefferson was chosen to draw up a declaration of independence, and John Adams and Benjamin Franklin were members of the committee to which the draft would be submitted for approval. News came on July 2 that Congress had voted to accept the declaration.

It was announced throughout the city that the text of the declaration would be read to the public in the State House yard on July 8. In the early afternoon Peale joined the solemn and expectant crowd that gathered around the observatory platform. John Nixon, ardent patriot and former city alderman, mounted the ladder to the platform and in a strong, ringing voice read the deathless words of the Declaration of Independence, beginning:

When, in the Course of human events, it becomes necessary for one people to dissolve the political bands which have connected with another. . . .

We hold these truths to be self-evident: That all men are created equal; that they are endowed by their Creator with certain unalienable Rights; that among these are Life, Liberty and the pursuit of Happiness.

Following the statement of the principles of liberty came the grievances against Great Britain, protests against which had gone unheeded, making revolution inevitable.

When Nixon finished reading, a sigh seemed to rise from the people, a sigh of relief. Now the colonies knew where they stood. Then came a roar of acclamation.

A boy had been stationed in the yard to give the signal when the reading was completed. He ran to the foot of the belfry and shouted to the old bell ringer, "Ring! Ring!" And the bronze bell, cast in England in 1753 and prophetically inscribed "Proclaim Liberty throughout the land to all the inhabitants thereof," seemed to shout, "Liberty!

Liberty! Liberty!" The colonies had broken with the mother country irrevocably.

Men rushed to the courtroom on the second floor of the State House and tore the insignia of Britain from above the judge's bench. The elaborate carving was thrown into one of the many bonfires that had been lighted; the lion and the unicorn writhed in the leaping flames. For two hours the State House bell rang on, a joyful sound to the ears of patriot Whigs, a voice of doom to Loyalists. Church bells chimed in, and crisp salutes of musket fire added to the happy noise. When darkness fell, patriots set candles in their windows, which threw a soft light on the faces of the people who, forming impromptu parades, marched through the streets. The spirit of carnival persisted until midnight when suddenly a noise like the low roll of distant cannon was heard. A hush fell over the crowds; faces paled. Was it the British? Then a vivid flash of lightning zigzagged across the sky and huge raindrops began to fall. The noise had been thunder! The citizens scampered to their homes as rain pelted down. Some of them had sober thoughts of the task before them. Independence could be made reality only at the cost of bloodshed and sacrifice.

15

Artist into Soldier

AFTER THE STORM brought the celebration to an abrupt end, Peale, who had been enjoying the noisy demonstration, walked home slowly. Paying no attention to the teeming rain, he tried to reach a decision. Obviously it was the duty of every able-bodied patriot to fight for the liberty of his country. What was his own obligation? He abhorred violence; he was just getting settled into a promising career in a new place; he was thirty-five, no longer young; he had a big family to support; on the other hand, his conscience told him——

When he walked into his home, his mind was made up. Late as it was, Rachel was waiting up for him. She looked like a child in her linsey-woolsey robe, with two dark braids hanging down her back and a ruffled nightcap set saucily on her head. Scolding him, she pulled off Charly's soaking coat, wrapped a shawl around him, fetched slippers for his wet feet, and brewed a cup of hot sassafras tea. As he sipped it, he told her that he had decided to enlist.

Rachel was appalled. "But Charly, what about all the orders you have taken? You must fill them. I pray you, wait until they are completed and then"—her voice broke—

119

"enlist if you feel you must." Peale agreed that it was sound advice and promised to devote every hour to finishing his commissions.

August 9, 1776, he enlisted in the Philadelphia "Associators," a volunteer organization which was pledged to defend the city. In accordance with a plan suggested by Benjamin Franklin, the "Associators" elected their officers from the ranks.

Charles was assigned at once to night watch. Mrs. Peale and Rachel foresaw an immediate attack by the redcoats on their dear Charly and pressed a heavy blanket on him to keep him from perishing of the cold on a warm August night.

Mrs. Peale asked Charly to go with her on an unexplained errand to Barrister Charles Carroll, who was now a member of Congress. As they walked along, he was proud of his handsome mother in her Sunday-best gray gown. She was still young and vigorous at sixty-seven. Carroll received them cordially, and Mrs. Peale stated her errand. Would he arrange to have Charly excused from military service?

Her son, ordinarily soft-voiced and courteous, shouted wrathfully, "If I did not serve personally, I would never let the sun shine on my head again! Believe me, sir, I knew nothing of Mother's intention in coming here. Surely you will not think me capable of such cowardice. Mother, how could you shame me so!"

Mrs. Peale, her face as white as her snowy lace cap, explained in a shaking voice, "I am afraid for his safety, but that is not what worries me most. What will his family live on if he goes to war? We have nothing but what he earns by painting. You know, Mr. Carroll, what hard times we have had in the past. What can we do now with four little children?"

Carroll soothed her as best he could. "It will not be for long, Mrs. Peale; the militia term is short and he will soon be free again. Charles is a good patriot, we need more like him."

A contingent of Maryland militia moved through Philadelphia on its way to defend the Hudson River at New York. With it came Ensign James Peale and Captain Nathaniel Ramsay who had a brief reunion with the family, while Peale shopped for the captain, purchasing regimentals and a gold-laced hat. Soon after their departure St. George came up from Annapolis on a mission for the Commissary for Military Supplies. His job was to organize a system of supply for the army without adequate funds. He was an officer in the Maryland militia, and had been selected for this difficult task because of his reputation as an able business executive. Mrs. Peale was proud that her sons were doing their patriotic duty but frankly fearful for their safety.

Anxiety was in the air, and crowds gathered to read the bulletins that were hastily printed and posted throughout the city when news was brought by dispatch riders. General Howe and his redcoats had landed on Long Island. . . . Washington had evacuated New York. . . . Continental Army defeated on Washington Heights. . . . The Americans were retreating. . . . The Continental Army had crossed over into New Jersey. . . . The Americans were retreating.

The rebel forces retreated across New Jersey with the

British so close at their heels that the two armies could hear each other's bands. Philadelphia, key city of the states, was gravely endangered. Feverish defense activity gripped the capital. Cannon, which were placed along the shores of the Delaware to guard against attack by water, boomed dully as the artillery practiced. Some infantrymen perfected their marksmanship on Centre Square while others, well out of range of fire, were drilled in the manual of arms. David Rittenhouse, for the Committee of Safety, called militia officers to proceed to Philadelphia bringing as many wagons as they could command. Men and boys eagerly read recruiting posters, which contained the glittering promises made by recruiting posters throughout the ages:

A bounty of twelve dollars, and annual and fully sufficient supply of good and handsome cloathing, a daily allowance of a large and ample ration of provisions, together with sixty dollars a year in gold and silver money . . . the opportunity of spending a few happy years in viewing the different parts of this beautiful continent.

The posters usually described the return of the soldier with "pockets full of money and his head covered with laurels," words that would be recalled as bitter mockery by the ragged, ill-fed, seldom-paid men who fought the battles of the Revolution.

Peale's block of the city militia elected him second lieutenant; his conscientious attention to his responsibilities quickly won him a first lieutenancy. Foreseeing, as the battle front neared Philadelphia, that the militia would be called into action, Peale visited the homes of his men. He made a list of the necessities their families would require when the men were away, for the militia had some funds for the assistance of the families of its poorer members. He reassured the wives and mothers by promising to supply what their men would need in the field. This thoughtfulness not only kept the company intact but added new recruits, bringing the number up to eighty. Kindness did more to keep Peale's group together than the stern discipline of other officers.

Washington's retreat toward the Delaware continued. His army decreased each day, for the soldiers, enlisted in the militia for a short term, blithely returned home to take up their personal affairs when the term ended. If the general had had funds to pay a bonus for re-enlistment, he might have been able to keep many men, but Congress had not voted funds for that purpose. By the time he reached Trenton, his army had dwindled to three thousand men. He was followed by a large, well-fed and well-armed British army reinforced with hired Hessian troops.

Thomas Paine, who had volunteered for army service soon after the publication of "Common Sense," had been part of the disheartening retreat across New Jersey. Knowing the immense difficulties which Washington faced as a result of the fluctuations in the number of his troops, he published an appeal to the patriots for more heroic efforts. He warned that greater perseverance was required, saying, "These are the times that try men's souls. The summer soldier and the sunshine patriot will, in this crisis, shrink from the service of his country, but he who stands it now deserves the loyal thanks of men and women."

Philadelphia, only thirty miles from Trenton, was panic-stricken. Gaunt, ragged soldiers, with pitiful tales of hardship and exaggerated estimates of British strength, streamed into Philadelphia, bringing with them the sick and wounded. These evidences of the horror of war fed the rising fears. Shopkeepers boarded up their shops and joined the rush to the country, which seemed to offer greater safety.

Peale thought it wise to send his family out of town and secured space with a farmer's family in Abingdon, twelve miles to the north. He secured wagons to transport them and their possessions. Of course, he sent along the model's chair, his painting equipment, and paintings for safekeeping. It was December 5, and a heavy snow was falling as the wagons started slowly down the street. Peale looked after them until they were hidden by a thick curtain of white. He was haunted by Rachel's eyes which had seemed to say, "Shall we never be together? May we never stay in one place for a little while?"

It was well for his peace of mind that Charles did not know that another family had moved in with the same farmer at Abingdon. Fortunately, they were acquainted with the Peales. Margaret Jane welcomed the opportunity to exercise her gift for organization. While she was arranging a living schedule that would offer the minimum of friction, a curious flock of sheep wandered through the open kitchen door. This ridiculous addition to the crowd already in the house made everyone laugh, creating a friendly atmosphere at the onset of a difficult situation. The household, even without the sheep, was so large that a maid stood at the hearth all day making buckwheat cakes for the hungry group.

After saying good-by to his family, Peale prepared to lead his men to the battle front. They were part of the

Second Battalion, whose uniform consisted of a dark brown coat with green facings, white vest and breeches, white stockings, and half boots. With this outfit Peale wore a tricorn hat ornamented with a gold button and gold lace and heavy fur gloves to protect his hands. Besides his rifle, he carried a thin mattress and a blanket, a change of linen, materials for small paintings, and a little cask of rum. The rum was not for his own use—he preferred water—but for his men in emergencies. Peale was not a warlike figure; his slight frame, kind expression, and soft voice gave no outward indication of the moral strength and physical fortitude he possessed. He was a considerate father rather than a domineering officer to his men.

A fleet of small boats was waiting to carry the troops up the Delaware toward Trenton. The Pennsylvania militia embarked first, followed by veterans of the Massachusetts campaign. The snow was still falling, the wind was icy. Peale advised his men to make beds of the army tents which were distributed among the boats. The next morning they improvised sails from the tents to hasten their slow progress up the river.

At noon, December 7, they landed on the New Jersey shore. But Washington had decided to make the Delaware River his defense line; all troops were ordered back to Pennsylvania. For seventy miles up and down the river, the general had commandeered every craft from canoes to barges to transport his army and to leave the British without means to cross the river.

It was a wild scene. Strong Massachusetts fishermen maneuvered the odd assortment of boats. Cannon, wagons, and horses were loaded on the barges; the horses, neighing and cavorting, were driven aboard with shouts and curses. Tattered Continentals filled the smaller craft, the wind whistling through their pitiful rags. Great watch fires on both shores illuminated the operation. As the last boat reached the Pennsylvania shore, the British marched into Trenton and occupied the town.

Peale's heart was torn by the sight of the hungry, almost naked men who had made the long retreat across New Jersey. He looked for James and Nathaniel; they should be among the troops. Two ragged creatures came up to him. He was surprised when one of them called him "Charly." Then he recognized James, hatless, his hair a wild tangle, his face blotched with sores, his only garment a filthy blanket coat. The second scarecrow was Nathaniel Ramsay, his uniform torn and muddy, his face blackened by powder, and the lovely gold-laced hat gone forever. Peale secured clothes for them from the militia supplies, bathed James's face and applied an ointment, and thanked God that he had found them alive.

While the troops were being reformed, drilled, and readied for action on the Pennsylvania shore, news came that Congress had decided to continue its session in Baltimore on December 20. There was heated discussion of this move. Some called it cowardice; others thought it wisdom. Peale, pointing out that Congress would have to disband if the British took Philadelphia, inquired how a new body could be elected. Ramsay reasoned that a city in fear of capture, rife with the wildest rumors, was no place for calm deliberation. Washington had warned Congress that the British intended to take Philadelphia, "Happy would I be, if I could see the means of preventing them; at present I

confess I do not." The Whigs approved the move; to the
Loyalists it seemed a confession of weakness and they grew
bold and arrogant.

In the midst of military duties and general confusion,
Peale found time to make small portraits of three officers.
He had remarkable powers of concentration and saw no
reason why he should not pursue his profession whenever
it was possible to do so.

But he would have to lay down his brushes, for action
was at hand. Cornwallis, contemptuous of the ragged Continentals whose numbers dwindled constantly, left an out-
post of Hessians at Trenton and a few nearby points and
started toward New York to establish winter quarters. No
self-respecting army would think of fighting during the
winter months. But Washington had stiffened the morale
of his troops. He raised the pay of officers and offered
bonuses to those who would re-enlist so that he could hold
the experienced men, though he did not yet know where
he would get the money to fulfill his promises. With these
inducements and the inspiring quality of his personality,
he had built up his forces to five thousand men.

Before the Delaware could freeze over and make an icy
bridge for the redcoats to cross, Washington issued orders
for a brilliant strategic move in which Peale would play a
modest part.

16

In the Field of Battle

O<small>N</small> C<small>HRISTMAS</small> E<small>VE</small>, 1776, in a blinding snowstorm, twenty-five hundred of Washington's troops were ferried across the Delaware River to New Jersey. From dark to dawn the Massachusetts seamen navigated the miscellaneous craft through the perilous waters, landing one boatload and turning back at once for another and another. Upon landing, the men were formed into companies and were ordered to march to Trenton. Washington's plan was to catch the Hessians off guard in the midst of their Christmas celebration.

> *On Christmas Day, in seventy-six,*
> *Our gallant troops with bayonets fixed*
> *To Trenton marched away.*

Washington was right. The homesick Hessians, who had been drinking heavily for hours, were overwhelmed by the sudden attack and were forced to surrender. With a thousand prisoners and welcome military stores, Washington recrossed the Delaware to Pennsylvania.

But Peale had no part in the victory at Trenton. The Second Pennsylvania Battalion and the seasoned New England militia, under the command of John Cadwalader, did not cross with Washington's contingent. They had been ordered to proceed to Bristol ferry, cross there, and approach Trenton from the opposite direction. The storm had reached such furious intensity when they reached the ferry that crossing was out of the question.

They did not get across the Delaware until the twenty-seventh. Taking only what they could carry on their backs, they marched to Bordentown in the direction of Trenton, their officers blissfully unaware that Washington's forces had returned to Pennsylvania and that they alone faced the enemy in New Jersey. However, the British who were guarding Bordentown fled to Princeton when they heard of the defeat of the Hessians at Trenton; the way was clear for the Pennsylvania and New England troops. Since they were marching without supplies, the first concern at Bordentown was to find food and shelter for the weary soldiers. Peale recorded his own success in his diary:

Dec. 28. My co[mpan]y got quarters where some Kings Troops had been & left them full of Hay and very Dusty. I ordered them to be cleaned and taking a walk I found a Store House and wrote on it Kings Stores delivering out. I got ¼ Beef and some Pork. I then heard of some Flower & went & got a barrel. . . . I went to desire a Family to let a negro girl make up some bread for us. The Lady of the House told me she would do it herself.

The men were just beginning to relax when "we were ordered immediately to march and having no Wagon we could not bring our Flower." Four miles of marching brought them to Crosswick, where things were in a lamentable state for "The Hessians have taken Hogs, Sheep, Horses and Cows everywhere, even children have been stripped of their Cloathes. The abuse of the inhabitants is beyond description." They did not linger in that Hessian-made desert but plodded on to Trenton. On January 2, 1777, Peale wrote:

At one Oclock this morning began a march for Trent Town. The roads are very muddy, almost over our Shoe Tops. The Number of Troop and the Badness of the Way, so many Runs to cross and fences to Remove, make it a very tedious march. The sun had risen more than an hour before we reached the Town. After, the difficulty of geting quarters kept us a long time under arms.

Quarters were found and Peale, stretched out on a plank, was catching a nap when the call to arms came. The British were approaching. Cornwallis, astonished by the success of the "contemptible rebels" at Trenton, had returned from New York to give battle.

In the meantime, Washington, invested by Congress with the powers of a military dictator, had brought four thousand troops to Trenton. Now, on January 2, 1777, the Continental Army and the militiamen were ordered to muster on the parade ground, and Peale was "greatly struck by the appearance of so fine an army. 4 Brigades at least parade in the same field below the town."

That afternoon the Americans engaged the British. At the first onslaught of the crack troops, the less-experienced Continental infantry fell back, but the American artillery raked the enemy lines with such fierce fire that the redcoats retreated. At the sight of this welcome withdrawal, the rebels shouted for joy. The loudness of their cheers convinced the British that they faced a larger force than they had thought, and they prudently ceased hostilities as darkness fell. The light of many American campfires gave the enemy a view of preparations for defense and of men furiously digging trenches. The British decided that they could safely rest until morning. What they did not know was that behind this camouflage Washington was withdrawing his army to Princeton. A thaw had made the roads a sea of mud, but a sudden drop in temperature hardened the roads by evening so that the caissons could roll and the men could step along at a brisk pace. It seemed a miracle.

When the crisp, cold day dawned, the British charged the defense line they had observed the night before, but they found no one to fight. There was nothing but a line of dying fires and freshly dug trenches. In a rage at this trick, the redcoats hurried to the Princeton road where the first contingent of Continentals was ready with loaded muskets. But they were not ready for the savage bayonet attack launched by the British, and the line broke, the men fleeing in terror. However, the next line, led by Washington himself, moved up. It consisted of the New England veterans and the Pennsylvania militia; Peale was in their midst:

I carried my platoon to the top of the hill and fired and then retreated Loading. We returned to the charge & fired a 2nd time & retreated as before. The third time coming up, the Enemy began to retreat. I must here give the New England boys their due . . . they stood the fire without regarding the balls which whistled their thousand different notes around our heads.

The larger part of the British force retreated to New Brunswick, which was an important depot for their stores, but many fled to Princeton and made Nassau Hall, which housed the College of New Jersey, their headquarters. Washington brought up his artillery, and the first cannon ball hurtled through a window of the chapel and hit the head in a portrait of George II, leaving the ornate gold frame undamaged. Like the portrait of their former king, the redcoats lost their heads and surrendered to the rebels. Jubilantly Peale wrote, "A flag was sent and we huzared victory."

The cheers were stilled when orders came to march out from Princeton to halt fresh troops sent by Cornwallis. The men had not slept for thirty-six hours; they were utterly weary and worn after days of marching and fighting. The roads had again softened into deep mud. Peale's company sat down by the roadside and refused to go on. He reasoned with them without success. Then he urged them on with promises of food and shelter. That brought them to life:

We continued on our way perty briskly . . . then pushed on to a Tavern a little further and got them into a Loft amidst a fine heap of straw. Now they laid down and most of them was asleep in a few moments so sound I could not get a single man to go with me to get Provisions. I had the promise of a barrel of Flower and had the lent of an oven but could get nobody to assist me in bringing it to be Bak'd. Then I went to a House further in town & purchased some Beef which I got a good Woman to boil against I should call for it in the morning. And I got a small kettle full of Petatoes boiled where we lodged [the tavern]. I then layed me down to rest among the men on the Hessian straw and thought myself happy tho' the room was full of Smoak as if to cure Bacon.

It was characteristic that Peale, just as weary as his men, could not rest until he had procured food for his company. Recalling these war experiences, he wrote in his memoirs:

Peale was a thin, spare, pale-faced man, in appearance totally unfit to endure the fatigues of long marches and of laying on the cold, wet ground, sometimes covered by snow. Yet . . . he endured this campaign better than many others, whose appearance was more robust. He always carried a piece of dryed Beef in his pocket and water in his canteen which he found was better than rum.

The next morning his men tumbled out of the straw rested and refreshed. Peale led them to the house of the "good Woman" to get the beef she had cooked for them. The men were squatted along the roadside, eating the stew with evident relish, when General Washington rode up. Reining in his horse, he asked Peale why the company had not yet begun to march.

"Your Excellency," explained Peale, "I had these victuals cooked to give my men the strength to march. They must eat to be able to fight."

He looked so earnest in his concern for his soldiers that Washington could not help smiling as he said, "Very well then, but march ahead as fast as you can." He touched his horse with a spur and, still smiling no doubt, cantered down the road.

During the march the men complained that the frozen, rutted roads had cut their shoes to pieces and that their feet were gashed and bleeding. Lieutenant Peale, full of sympathy, obtained two cowhides from which he fashioned moccasins for the men who were worst off, turning the fur side in for greater warmth. He was grateful for his ability to work leather, which was learned in the saddlery business. The whole army needed shoes. Peale learned later that Washington could have taken New Brunswick with its valuable stores if his men had had shoes adequate to the march.

Instead the army limped painfully to Morristown, which the commander in chief had selected for winter quarters. As Peale walked along with his company, he was joined by a Philadelphia physician, Dr. Benjamin Rush. He was one of the few doctors with the army, as little provision had been made for caring for the sick and wounded. Rush shocked Charles by criticizing Congress for not properly supporting Washington and admitted that he was pessimistic about the outcome of the war. Peale, always hopeful, disagreed with him, feeling certain that Washington would win the struggle. On one subject they agreed heartily, that it was shameful that the wounded received no organized attention. Peale's own men needed care, and he did not know where to get help for them.

At Morristown Peale found good quarters for his company and was fortunate enough to discover two medical men, Doctors Cochrane and Johnson, who gave him medicines and instructions on how to use them. He dosed his casualties and nursed them himself. He obtained another cowhide and cut it carefully so that he could make the largest number of moccasins from it. Doctoring and cobbling did not fully occupy his time; he painted a miniature of one of the officers. The army rejoiced at the news that Cornwallis was withdrawing his armies toward New York; rest from battle was at hand for the weary rebels.

The enlistment term of the Philadelphia militia expired on January 11, 1777, and Peale and his company went home. Short militia terms were a curse to Washington. The men were scarcely trained and experienced before their

COLONEL WASHINGTON   (1772)
Washington and Lee University

LAFAYETTE (1777)
Reproduced by permission of the Virginia Historical Society

SELF-PORTRAIT IN THE UNIFORM OF THE PHILADELPHIA BRI(
(1777–1778)
American Philosophical Society

period of enlistment ended and they departed to take up their private lives. Pay in paper money offered no inducement to remain in service. Washington lacked hard cash until Robert Morris, the Philadelphia merchant whose portrait Peale had painted, raised $50,000 in coin on the security of his honor and reputation. Morris wrote to Washington, "I was up early to despatch a supply of $50,000. to your Excellency. It gives me great pleasure you have engaged the troops to continue." Morris had saved the army. Washington could now make good his promises of better pay for officers and rewards for re-enlistment. Paper money issued by Congress, which had no gold basis, was looked on with suspicion. But when the news got around that pay in hard money was available, it brought recruits and encouraged militiamen to return to service. The soldiers agreed with Tom Paine who said, "Money is money and paper is paper and all the inventions of man cannot make it otherwise."

Peale's first thought when he left the army was to rescue his family from the crowded farmhouse at Abingdon and return to Philadelphia now that the city was safe from invasion. The move was greeted with joy, for not even Margaret Jane's diplomacy had kept tempers from wearing thin in the crowded household. The discomforts of bumping over the frozen, rutted roads were borne with cheerful patience. And when the Peales and all their possessions arrived at the house on Market Street that Charly had rented, they compared it to a palace. Three-year-old Raphaelle and his little sister Angelica ran about the house making noise freely after weeks of "Hush!" and "Don't!" Peale thought they were like birds freed from a cage.

During the remainder of the winter, Peale rode frequently to Morristown to visit his brother James and Nathaniel Ramsey, who were encamped with Maryland troops. He met Mrs. Martha Washington again, for she had joined her husband at his headquarters in Freeman's Tavern. She did much to improve the lot of the sick and wounded, organizing canteens at which the men could get hot food and inducing wives of officers and the women of Morristown to sew clothing for the soldiers and to knit socks for their freezing feet.

With little to give his men but the glory of their past victories, Washington communicated his own hope and confidence to the army, gradually bettering conditions, placing his best officers where they would be most effective, overseeing the training of new officers, and in general bringing the forces to their highest efficiency up to that time.

In the winter of 1777 the better part of Peale's time was spent in Philadelphia where he became entangled, thanks to his popularity, in various political coils.

17

"Fit and Painted
Painted and Fit"

AFTER THE PUBLICATION of the Declaration of Independence each state was faced with the problem of forming its own government. Dissension divided the patriot Whigs of Philadelphia. On one side the Quakers, the Pennsylvania Germans, and the wealthy were conservative and cautious, while the small landowners, tradesmen, and intellectuals were radical and sometimes violent in their political convictions. The divergence was sharply evident in the attitude of the two groups toward the approved constitution, which provided a one-chamber legislature, following the pattern of the former governing body, the assembly.

The conservatives felt that a one-chamber body elected directly by the people would have too much unchecked power, and they wanted to call a convention to revise the constitution. The radical Whigs believed that the accepted constitution should be put into effect; it carried a provision that it could be amended after seven years if desired. To them it seemed inadvisable to change what had been made law.

The radical group formed the Whig Society, a loosely organized discussion group. Peale, a convinced Constitutionalist, attended one of the meetings which was held at a nearby school, to see what it was like. The meeting had not yet been called to order, for no one was willing to serve as chairman.

Peale, disgusted by the wrangle that was going on, rose and announced, "I fail to see why men should be unwilling to take the trouble to keep order in an assembly of their fellow citizens." He scarcely had time to sit down before he was unanimously elected chairman. After his rash little speech he could hardly decline the offer.

With Peale in the chair the meeting got under way, the speakers criticizing in abusive terms the attitude of the conservatives and offering arguments in favor of the constitution as it stood. One man quoted an anecdote which Benjamin Franklin had used to show the dangers of a two-chamber legislature. It was about a snake with two heads and one body which was going to a brook to drink. In passing under a hedge, the snake's progress was obstructed by a thick stem. One head wanted to go to the right and the other to the left, and so much time was spent in argument that the snake died of thirst.

Peale remained chairman of the Whig Society, for he believed in the peaceful settlement of disputes. But the conflict about the constitution, which raged for nearly ten years, stirred political controversies that were more violent than those in any other state. Thus Peale was caught up in a whirlwind which disturbed his life for years.

For the present he turned to a task much more to his liking. The Committee of Safety was gathering supplies for the army. The Committee encouraged the manufacture of gunpowder and weapons, induced women to roll bandages and pick lint, and among other things collected blankets for the troops. Peale was asked to canvass his district, which he did with outstanding success. His eyewitness stories of suffering in the camps lured warm coverings out of many a carved or painted chest.

During the winter of 1777 the city militia had been reorganized, and Peale, having expressed his willingness to serve again, received a commission as captain of the Fourth Company of the Fourth Battalion with a command of sixty men. The company was ordered into action on June 18, for the British were attempting to take New Jersey.

Early that morning Charly went to market to get provisions for the household. Rachel was not well, and he wanted to spare her that task. After depositing the heaping basket in his kitchen, he bade the family good-by and led his men to Washington's camp in New Jersey. When they neared the camp, they had a view of it from the top of a hill, which the artist-captain described in his diary:

One of the most lovely prospects I have ever seen. Overlooking an extensive Country which appeared perty level and finishing [with] Mountains of different distances. This level appeared like an Infinite number of Fine Gardens . . . all varigated with the several Coulers of approaching Harvest. . . . From this Hill we could see where Genl. Washington was encamped, also several of our encampments and at about 4 or 5 miles, the Encampment of the Enemy on the Hills by Summerset Court House.

There were no orders for Peale's company when it reached the camp, for the British were retreating. Charles chafed at this waste of time. Why not use it in painting another portrait of Washington? He went to the general's headquarters and asked him to pose, but Washington, quite understandably, refused. The visit was not entirely fruitless, for "Genl. Washington gave me an invitation to dine with him next day." The prospective guest at once prepared for the event, "I am obliged to get some linnen washed to appear desent at Genl. Washington's." When he went to collect his laundry the next morning, he discovered that his horse had disappeared. Peale seemed to have an affinity for runaway horses. He searched for the animal, getting hotter and dustier every minute, without success. He offered a soldier a dollar to take up the hunt, but when the wandering horse was finally captured, it was too late to get to headquarters for dinner. It was annoying but there was no need to waste any time.

Began a miniature of Coll Stone at a Log House without a Window. The Time proving Rainey, I stayed at this House 2 nights and painted the Likeness of Major Starrett as well as finishing Coll. Stone. I now determined to Return Home, having now lost all Hopes of Seeing an Engagement. And my impatience to see my Family was so great that I could not with any Pleasure stay to take the likeness of Genl. Washington and others who made application to me.

Militia officers had the privilege of returning home for brief visits if the army was not actively engaged. The commander in chief, who in an emergency often found many officers missing, disapproved of the practice. But Peale, who evidently was concerned about his family, availed himself of the privilege and remained in Philadelphia from July to early August, profitably employed in painting several portraits.

Then came the news that General Howe had sailed up the Chesapeake and was landing his troops at the head of the bay. Washington moved his army to Wilmington to intercept the British on their way to Philadelphia. On August 24 the Continental Army, now 10,000 strong, crossed the Schuylkill River on a bridge constructed of boats and marched through Philadelphia under the recently adopted flag. The new flag retained the thirteen alternating red and white stripes, but in the upper corner a blue field with a circle of thirteen white stars replaced the British Union Jack. Washington rode at the head of the troops, a commanding figure on his fine charger, and at his side was a slender young Frenchman, the Marquis de Lafayette, who had come to assist the Americans in their fight for freedom. His coming was doubly welcome because of the good supply of gunpowder he brought with him. For two days the army streamed across the city, marching smartly to a lively tune, "Yankee-Doodle." The soldiers wore uniforms of every color, shabby and dirty for the most part; some wore deerskin hunting coats; few were dressed in the blue-and-buff uniform of the Continental Army. But no matter how nondescript their dress, the men carried themselves like soldiers and their guns were clean and highly polished.

The shrill notes of fifes, the roll of drums and the impressive parade of soldiers aroused the patriotism of the Whigs of Philadelphia, and they decided to control the Loyalists in their midst. A committee was formed, which was to surprise the British sympathizers with a demand to pledge themselves not to act against the government. If they refused, they were jailed. Peale was made a member of the committee, and he found it a hateful chore. Many of the Loyalists had been his friends and patrons; he was horrified to find the name of his one-time benefactor, James Tilghman, on his list. Peale remembered only that Tilghman had lent him money with which to start his saddlery business; he forgave the threat of arrest that came later. He approached his old friend on the delicate errand with great reluctance, and it took hours of persuasion to get Tilghman's promise to "stay in his house and do nothing in anyway injurious to the free states of Northern America." Long afterward Peale wrote, "It will readily be imagined how much Peale was pleased to have the affair got over with."

Meanwhile Washington had taken his stand on the Brandywine, a wide creek that flows into the Delaware River at Wilmington. There he waited until September 11, when he crossed the stream to meet the oncoming waves of redcoats. The rebels drove the British back with two fierce assaults but then, greatly outnumbered, fled in confusion, and Washington could not rally them. Under cover of darkness he withdrew his forces to Chester, halfway between Wilmington and the capital. He was criticized for engaging the large British army at the Brandywine, but he felt that the patriots would not have forgiven him had he let the enemy take Philadelphia unopposed. On September 27 the British occupied the city. General Howe and his troops were given an elaborate welcome by the Loyalists and were entertained lavishly throughout the winter.

While these events were in the making, Captain Peale had rejoined his company at Fort Billingsport, just outside Philadelphia. But when occupation seemed certain, he used his officer's prerogative to take a brief leave to get his family to safety. He had a good spot in mind and hurried home to move his family there. It was evening when he reached the city and found the windows of his house shuttered. He pounded on the doors but received no response. Neighbors had seen the Peales drive off in a big wagon with considerable baggage, but no one knew where they had gone. It was morning before the frantically worried man found someone who knew their destination. Learning that they had gone to Haddonfield, New Jersey, Peale hurried to the ferry, crossed to the opposite shore, and finally found his family. They were so frightened and confused that he could not bear to scold them for fleeing on their own initiative to a place he thought far from safe. For the moment he could do nothing about it; he had to return to his men at Fort Billingsport.

Before he reached the fort, a messenger intercepted him. Nathaniel Ramsay was desperately ill, and Margaret Jane wanted him to get medicine in Philadelphia and bring it without delay to a farm about fifteen miles north of the city where the Ramsays had taken refuge. His men would have to wait. The devoted brother ferried the river again, procured the medicine, and trudged out to the farm. Charles had walked twenty-five miles that day; he must have needed the bit of dried beef he always carried in his pocket!

At farmer Brittain's, where the Ramsays were staying, there were several unoccupied rooms. With the farmer's consent, Peale decided to bring his family there from New

Jersey; it seemed a safer location for them. Brittain obtained two light wagons—Ramsay's servant drove one and Peale the other—and the journey across the Delaware was made once more. The roads were clogged with Whigs who were escaping to the country, for the news had reached Philadelphia that the British were nearing the city. Rachel and Mrs. Peale were too fatigued and worried to protest being uprooted again. They were packed bag and baggage into the wagons, and the Delaware was crossed one more weary time. By the greatest good luck they found a barge to ferry them across to the Pennsylvania shore, for now panic was everywhere. The British were almost at the city gates. Their luck held as they drove, with all speed possible on the crowded roads, missing the oncoming enemy by only a mile or two. With infinite relief Peale saw his family safely under the Brittain roof. Without stopping to take a deep breath, he started off to rejoin his men at Billingsport. But by now the British were at the outskirts of Philadelphia, and it was impossible to get through. Back he went to Brittain's farm. He helped the farmer cast bullets and made himself useful by taking powder and shot to the Whigs who had taken refuge in the country.

On October 3 the sound of gunfire and cannonading was heard from the direction of Germantown, just outside Philadelphia. Peale took his gun, ammunition, and painting kit and hastened to the battle front. Washington had attacked the British outposts at Germantown, and his success seemed assured until a pea-soup fog descended upon the battlefield. In the chaos which followed, men shot at ghosts in the murk, often firing on their comrades. When the order to retreat came, the Americans could not understand it. They were certain that they were winning. Not until the fog lifted did the British know they had won the day; they saw the rebels retreating.

Peale arrived in the thick of the confusion and found himself with a contingent of Maryland troops. He searched for James. Looking fearfully at recumbent forms on the ground, he saw men he knew, wounded. He did what he could to alleviate their suffering and get help to them, heartsick at the dreadful toll of war. Finally he found James, on picket duty, and Nathaniel Ramsay, who had recovered sufficiently to rejoin his command. With this anxiety off his mind and with no chance of finding his company in the confusion of retreat, Peale made his way back to the Brittain farm. It was a difficult and dangerous trip in the midst of retreating rebels and advancing British. The place itself too close to Philadelphia to be safe, he must move his family deeper into the country.

With the same two wagons used in the trek from New Jersey, the Peales set forth again with their battered possessions, driving up into the lovely rolling hills of Bucks County. The foliage along the roads was bright with autumn yellows and reds and the hills were veiled in blue haze, but the Peales had eyes for just one thing—a safe shelter. They asked for lodging at each farmhouse they passed, but they were already filled with refugees. Finally they saw a stone house nestled in a hollow, looking safe and comfortable. Poor tired Rachel, her dark eyes enormous in her pale face, looked up at her husband and said, "Oh, Charly, if we could only stay there!" When they stopped, Mr. Van Arsdalen, a farmer, welcomed them cheerfully and his wife bustled out to herd the weary travelers into her spotless house.

Peale saw that here at Newtown his dear ones would be comfortable. With his mind at rest on that score, he left to search for his company. It was marching along with the army near Worcester, not far from Philadelphia, when he caught up to the group. His men greeted him with enthusiasm, showing their affection for him by borrowing small sums of money, amounts which he set down in his diary. Since no battle seemed imminent, Peale's thoughts turned to painting. He called upon Washington at his head-quarters in the Peter Wentz house in Worcester, asking for a sitting. Washington granted his request, and they retired to a small bedroom for privacy, Washington perching on the side of the bed because the light was good there. This miniature was to be a gift to Martha, and the general was ready to help Peale in making it a success. One of Peale's company remarked of his captain, admiringly, "He fit and painted, painted and fit."

On November 2 the army moved on to entrench itself at Whitemarsh, thirteen miles from Philadelphia, where Peale was put in command of a picket guard in a clammy, cold mill. One night, when he was off watch, he fell asleep with his right hand outside the blanket. Charly was frantic with worry when he awoke and discovered that his hand was frostbitten. Without the use of that hand, how could he go on painting? What could he do to make a living? He tried all remedies that were suggested and massaged it with hot vinegar at frequent intervals. Nothing helped. It was two months before he could make effective use of his hand, two months in which he suffered the depths of despair.

Soon afterward his term of enlistment ended, and he returned to Newtown. He was cheered by the love and solicitude of Rachel and his mother and happy to be with his enchanting children. The peaceful interlude was soothing to nerves strained by political conflicts and the anxieties incident to war.

18

An Artist at Valley Forge

His HAND GRADUALLY regained its usefulness while Charly rested in the comfortable Van Arsdalen home. The farm supplied plentiful food. There was little salt to season it, however, for that commodity was extremely scarce. When obtainable, it was sold for outrageous prices, which imposed a serious hardship on farmers who needed salt to cure their pork and beef.

There was no such comfort for the Continental Army. Washington had withdrawn his forces to winter quarters at Valley Forge, a site chosen because it lay on high ground and commanded roads which led to powder mills and gunsmithies. Added advantages were a good-sized stream for water supply and nearby farms from which food could be obtained. There the army was placed between the British in Philadelphia and Congress, now continuing its session at York, Pennsylvania. Not far away, at Lancaster, the Liberty Bell had been safely hidden.

The bleeding feet of the barefoot soldiers had reddened the snowy roads as they marched painfully to Valley Forge. No shelter awaited them there, and their first project was to build rough wooden barracks. The men pooled their garments to equip the working force, and those lucky enough to have shoes lent them to the workers. The log huts they constructed, fourteen by sixteen feet, had no floor. The bare ground was the soldier's bed, and fortunate was the man who had a blanket to wrap about him. Washington had a good stone house for headquarters but refused to live in it until the men had roofs over their heads. Martha Washington joined her husband at camp, and her devoted love sustained him in the months of discouragement and anxiety.

The prosperous farms that had been counted on for food supplies yielded little; the farmers were unwilling to accept Continental money in payment, which was all that Washington had to offer. Because precious metals had to be imported, no hard money could be minted by the United States during the Revolution, and British, French, and Spanish coins were scarce. The farmers preferred to sell their produce to the British, who had hard money to pay for it. As a result the poorly housed, insufficiently clad men at Valley Forge were starving. Congress promised supplies but seemed incapable of carrying out its promises. Washington wrote despairingly to Congress, "Soap, vinigar and other articles allowed by Congress we see none of. The first indeed we have little need for; few men having more than one shirt, some only one, some none at all."

Lack of food, exposure, and insanitary conditions in the camp caused sickness to sweep through the army, and hundreds of men died at Valley Forge in that black winter of 1778. That any were willing to endure the suffering of those winter months is a tribute to their loyalty to the cause of their newborn country and to the magnetism of Washington's personality. Though he inspired faith and confidence, he carried despair in his heart. The Quaker owner of the headquarters house came upon the general one day in a little thicket near the stream; he was on his knees, praying for guidance and courage.

At the Van Arsdalen farm Peale, though he could not manage a brush yet, found he was able to make cases for his miniatures and shoes for the whole household. But a new uncertainty came to disturb his nights. Bands of British and Loyalists roamed the countryside at night, searching houses for Whigs and dragging them off to prison. When warned that searching parties were on the prowl, Peale would take his dog, gun, and a warm blanket and spend the night hidden in the woods. One night the dog growled and a twig snapped nearby. Peale put his gun on the ready. A figure appeared. Luckily Peale held his fire, for it was the wife of his friend David Rittenhouse. The woods were full of Whigs hiding from the search parties. On another occasion Peale encountered Polly Wrench and her husband Jacob Rush, brother of Dr. Benjamin Rush. When daylight came after one of these uneasy vigils, Peale would rise from his bed of dry leaves, dust himself off, and start for the farmhouse, often shooting game on his way back.

Rachel always welcomed him tearfully, showing what a strain the nights were for her, and she grew increasingly uneasy as the raids occurred more frequently. One morning she flung herself at him as he entered, crying, "Charly, please go to Valley Forge and stay there. You'll be safe from the raiders. I am so afraid for you here."

MARY CLAYPOOLE PEALE (ABOUT 1782)
Amherst College

STAIRCASE GROUP (1795)
Philadelphia Museum of Art

EXHUMING
THE FIRST
AMERICAN
MASTODON
(1806)

The Peale Museum,
Baltimore, gift of
Mrs. Harry White

LAST PORTRAIT OF WASHINGTON   (1795)
The New-York Historical Society

JAMES MONROE   (1818)
Alexander Smith Cochran Collection, Philipse Manor, Yonkers

THE ARTIST IN HIS MUSEUM (1822)
The Pennsylvania Academy of the Fine Arts

Charly could see that sleepless nights were making her ill and agreed to go, not unwillingly, since his hand was now limber enough to allow him to paint. But first he rode to Trenton and bought a little of that rarity, salt, and a small quantity of the equally scarce tea for his family. For his own pleasure he purchased three French books, translations of Ovid. At Valley Forge he lived with the Ramsays. Nathaniel, now a lieutenant colonel, had been allotted a few rooms in a house, making it possible for Margaret Jane to join him. She was such a charming hostess that their rooms were much frequented by Maryland officers. Peale settled down with them, thankful that he need not take to the woods at night; his days busy with portrait orders.

Before the occupation of Philadelphia, Congress had commissioned Peale to paint a full-length portrait of General Washington. He now began work on it. Because canvas was unobtainable, he used linen mattress ticking. With customary ingenuity he contrived a stretcher for the large "canvas" which folded in three parts without creasing the fabric, permitting him to carry it on horseback. It was to travel many miles before it was completed. He worked at headquarters whenever the general had a little leisure to give him, and there he met the charming young Marquis de Lafayette whom he had seen riding beside Washington in Philadelphia. Peale tried out his French, which was not too rusty, but the rapid replies of the voluble marquis floored him at first. He made a sketch of Lafayette, a tall, lithe figure, the face rugged, heavy-jawed, lighted by lively brown eyes. Peale knew that Benjamin Franklin, Silas Deane, and Arthur Lee, who were abroad nego-

tiating for financial and military aid from the French
government, had received useful advice and letters of introduction to important men in France from Lafayette.
The possibility of such help was the sustaining hope of all
who were carrying the responsibility of the Revolution.

Peale painted a vast number of portraits that winter.
Many were commissioned by officers who sent the paintings home, knowing that they themselves might never return. As he worked at these paintings, an idea came to
Peale. Was this not an opportunity to make a record of the
outstanding personalities of the Revolution in a series
of small sketches which later could be enlarged to life
size? They could form a gallery of portraits which would
commemorate the heroes and leaders of the war. He set
to work making such a collection, using what time he had
after filling orders which were providing the Peale family with a living. Using small squares of linen, he painted
officers (American and foreign), statesmen, doctors,
clergymen, and men in general who were playing a part
in the struggle for freedom. He included a self-portrait
in uniform and tricorn hat, showing an attractive, intelligent face with alert blue eyes.

He made brief visits to Bucks County and while there
painted many replicas of the miniature of Washington
which he had made in the cramped little farmhouse room
the previous autumn. There were constant demands for
copies.

Charles needed diversion. He found it in making a
xylophone, a percussion instrument of tuned wooden slats
which produced mellow, woody tones when struck with
small hammers. The family choir, reduced to his mother,

Rachel, and himself, needed a supporting accompaniment.

February 22, 1778, Rachel gave birth to a boy. Named Rembrandt, he was destined to follow the calling of the great Dutch portraitist. Rachel and Charly now had three living children: four-year-old Raphaelle, Angelica, who was three, and the baby. Bright, pretty children, they were a joy to their parents in those anxious days. Rembrandt was baptized in a Presbyterian church; the Anglican church was now too closely associated with the Loyalists for the Whiggish Peales.

During his visits to Valley Forge, Peale became aware of a change coming over the army, which was being drilled and disciplined by Baron von Steuben, a Prussian officer of distinguished military achievement. Like Lafayette, he had come to America in 1777 to help the rebels in their struggle. Washington made him Inspector General of the army with the rank of major general. Peale often left his painting to stand beside the parade ground, amazed to see the precision in drill and military bearing which Baron von Steuben had effected in the troops.

On May 4, 1778, the Americans received glorious news that an alliance had been signed with the French, that the most powerful nation of Europe was coming to the aid of the United States. It signified that France recognized the United States as an independent nation, struggling now to free itself completely from the domination of Britain. Peale was at Valley Forge on the sixth when the alliance was celebrated with a review of troops and endless cheers for the French king. An onlooker said that he had "never seen such unfeigned and perfect joy as was discovered in every countenance." Lafayette beamed with pride in his nation, and Washington was encouraged. Six weeks later the British evacuated Philadelphia.

A peace commission sailed up the Delaware later in May, bringing terms on which the British Parliament had offered to end the war. But the French alliance had been signed while the commission was at sea; and having a powerful ally, the American Congress found the peace terms unacceptable. The commission learned upon its arrival in Philadelphia that Howe had returned to England, leaving General Clinton in command. Moreover, Clinton, after a council of war, had decided to evacuate Philadelphia and retire to hold New York and Rhode Island for the British. There was nothing left for the peace commission to do but to set sail for home, taking with it hundreds of Loyalists who found that the climate of Philadelphia was no longer good for their health.

The redcoats moved to New Jersey. Throngs of Loyalists went with them, encumbering the troop movement with their household goods and baggage, a serious handicap to the British withdrawal. They were unwanted, homeless, unhappy refugees who were repaid in abuse and neglect for the hospitality they had lavished on the occupation forces. Transporting possessions of the Loyalists was hindrance enough to the evacuation, but in addition the soldiers insisted upon taking vast quantities of loot with them. The baggage wagons almost outnumbered the men.

As the last of the redcoats clambered aboard the river boats and pushed off from the Pennsylvania shore, the Whigs who had taken refuge in the country streamed back to the capital city. Among the first to arrive was Charles Willson Peale.

19

The Cost
of Convictions

Farmer Van Arsdalen borrowed a horse and wagon from one of his neighbors which, with his own, provided transportation for the Peales' journey home. As Charles helped pack their possessions, scarred and battered after their various travels, into the wagons and found places for all members of the family amid the baggage, he thought they looked as shabby as their household goods. However they were in good health, and he fervently hoped he would not have to uproot them again. Rachel, longing for a settled life, echoed that hope with all her heart.

They started out on June 18, 1778. While the return home was an occasion for rejoicing, the journey through the ravaged countryside was heartbreaking. Everywhere neat fences had been torn up for firewood, the green wheat had been wantonly cut down by the Hessians. The Peale children wept at the sight of dead horses and cattle in the meadows, spitefully slaughtered by enemy soldiers. When Rachel saw beautiful country places such as John Dickinson's ruined, trees slashed, gardens uprooted, she cried, "I hate those vandals! I hope General Washington kills them, every one." A violent sentiment from gentle Rachel.

As they entered the city, the destruction was even more appalling because it was more concentrated. Peale wrote:

> We set out early this morning and got to Philadelphia at 12 oclock. The city appeared very little like what it used to be—all the fences and pailings of every kind were demolished, the Houses in general in the suburbs were pulled to pieces, I suppose for firewood, and many in the midst of the city left in ruins.

Window frames had been torn out; doors had been wrenched from their hinges; even shingled roofs had been plundered for firewood. A horrible stench assailed their nostrils. The streets of the once clean Quaker city were clogged with filth, and shimmering clouds of flies buzzed over the refuse. The lovely State House was in an indescribable condition after its use as prison and hospital for rebels captured at the Brandywine or Germantown, whom the British had treated with callous neglect. In the State House yard a great pit was full of dead horses and bodies of men who had escaped their miseries through death. When Congress returned to Philadelphia, its first meeting had to be postponed; even after two weeks of Herculean labors to clean it, the stink which hung about the State House was too sickening to be borne.

Peale was distressed when he heard that Dr. Franklin's house had been pillaged and his electrical apparatus carried off. The stories of looting by the enemy were endless. The Peales approached their home fearfully and were immensely relieved to find it little damaged, though it was unbelievably dirty. Mrs. Peale, Rachel, and the slaves immediately started to clean with furious energy, Betsey and Charlie Polk did as much work as the grownups, and Peggy Durgan did her best to keep the children from getting under foot. Charly worked hard to restore his painting room to order; he was pleased to find the revolving platform unharmed.

Within ten days news came of a victory over the British at Monmouth Court House, New Jersey. British forces, hampered by the refugees from Philadelphia, had been slowly moving across New Jersey toward New York, and Washington moved his army in a parallel line. On June 28 Washington ordered General Lee to attack. Contact with the enemy had hardly been made when Lee ordered a retreat. Washington appeared at that moment and gave Lee a tonguelashing before the troops, calling him a "damned poltroon." Then, rallying the troops, Washington led such a furious attack on the British that the redcoats retreated, straggling back in the direction of New York. Von Steuben was jubilant; the men he had trained fought like disciplined soldiers. His months of work at Valley Forge had achieved results which stood up under the stress of battle.

Meanwhile those who had fled Philadelphia during the British occupation flocked back. There were touching scenes when families were reunited and friends found each other after long separation or learned that there were those they would never meet again. It was easy to recognize the citizens who had stayed in the city; they were plump and rosy in contrast to the gaunt, pale individuals who had led a hunted life in the country. Bitter animosities sprang up. Loyalists who remained in Philadelphia were the objects of hatred, and chill stiffness greeted any Whig who was suspected of collaboration.

Loyalists amounting to one-fifth of the population having left Philadelphia, the city authorities acted quickly to confiscate their property and keep a rein on the Loyalists who had not fled. The Committee of Safety organized an agency to sell confiscated property, money from such sales to supply funds for the city administration since no taxes had been levied as yet. The very word "taxes" was anathema to the rebels. Confiscation agents were allowed 5 per cent of the sales they made, but there were some who enriched themselves by buying the property and re-selling it at handsome profits.

Popular and reliable Peale was appointed one of the agents. The task was unpleasant, for in the course of the investigations neighbor tattled on neighbor, loosing a flood of bitterness, recrimination, and revenge. Violence often accompanied seizure of property. On one occasion when agents, searching for papers in a fine private house, broke open a magnificent mahogany desk, Peale offered to send a cabinetmaker to repair it at his own expense. Peale was not among those who profited through the sale of property. He was far too honest to do such a thing and spoke of the confiscation proceedings as the "most difficult, laborious and disagreeable task I have ever undertaken." It was characteristic of him to fulfill such duties to the best of his ability. Their unpleasantness was no reason for sidestepping them.

While he was still in the midst of the confiscation business, word came from Annapolis that his brother St. George was dying. Peale made all possible haste but reached Annapolis only on the day before St. George died. He was proud that his brother was mourned by many friends, for St. George was an attractive, able person, a man of substance and property. The *Maryland Gazette* called this patriot, who had done his country exceptionally useful service on the Commission for Military Supplies, "ingenious and amiable."

Peale was anxious that his brother's funeral should comply with the pledge made by patriots to avoid unnecessary expense for last rites. In the colonies, even among the Puritans, the customary trappings of funerals were extravagant, often including a painted coat of arms for the hearse, black caparisons decorated with death's-heads for the horses, and full sets of mourning attire and mourning rings for all relatives. Peale was only partly satisfied with St. George's funeral:

His funeral was desent and not expensive unless in one article, the winding sheet, which was muslin .@ £4.10.0 per yard and bought contrary to my advice by the person who had undertaken the management of these customary Peagentrys.

Back in Philadelphia, Charles took up the work of the confiscation agency again; but he relieved the strain by the happier task of making a mezzotint plate of his latest miniature of Washington. Prints from it were advertised for sale at John Dunlop's shop on Market Street. The price, five dollars each, was not high considering the depreciated currency of the time. A generous and friendly Spanish gentleman, Don Juan de Mirailles, purchased four dozen of the Washington prints to send abroad. Don Juan, an immensely wealthy man, had come from Cuba to make a report on the American Revolution for the Spanish government, which was considering alliance with the United States. De Mirailles, a colorful figure, was splendidly dressed. Magnificent diamonds sparkled on his beringed hands and in his knee buckles. He was a genial and open-handed man who had taken a great liking to Peale. He lent Charles one of his fine horses when Peale was obliged to make another trip to Annapolis—this time to execute the will of Rachel's mother, Mrs. Brewer.

As Charles rode along past Wilmington, he was aware that a nondescript mongrel dog kept following him, and when he dined at an inn before taking a ferry across the Susquehanna, he fed the faithful creature. In the bustle of getting aboard and tying Don Juan's horse securely, he lost sight of his four-footed friend until, arriving at Havre de Grace on the Maryland shore, he put up at an inn near the landing:

After I had been some time over the ferry, the Dogg came Runing into the House, panting and trembling with fateague & cold. He had swam the River which is one mile and a quarter wide. Poor Animal! I feed him and took him into the bed Room with me. He certainly deserves to be loved and made much of. He shall never want a good meal while I have it myself.

Just before Peale reached Baltimore, a carriage came rumbling along toward him, raising a cloud of dust. As he drew abreast of it, a veiled head appeared at the window and a feminine voice cried, "Mr. Peale! Mr. Peale!" It was Mrs. Washington on her way to Philadelphia to join her husband who was then conferring with Congress. Charles pulled up his horse and paused for a little chat, while the "Dogg" stretched out, glad of a chance to rest.

Mrs. Washington explained, "The general is trying to persuade Congress that we should only fight to defend ourselves. What do you think, Mr. Peale?"

"I agree with the general; we rebels only want our freedom. Let Britain give us that and we shall be glad to stop fighting."

With a touch of his whip the coachman started the horses. The carriage creaked along. Charles, with the dog close behind, rode on to Annapolis.

Mrs. Washington and Peale met again in Philadelphia on December 17, 1778, when the city gave a magnificent and costly reception for her. Her husband deplored the expenditure. He was still short of funds for carrying on the war, valuable officers were resigning for lack of pay, and yet vast sums were being spent for lavish entertainments. The cost of the banquet tendered to M. Gérard, the first French minister to the United States, was enough to have furnished the army with shoes. When Washington heard about another dinner at which 160 dishes were served, he thought sadly of his poor soldiers who never were sufficiently supplied with food.

Perhaps he disapproved of another state expenditure in which Peale figured. According to *The Pennsylvania Packet* of February 11, 1779:

His Excellency Gen. Washington, set off from this city to join the army in New Jersey. During the course of his short stay, the only relief he has enjoyed from his service since he first entered it; he has been honored with every mark of esteem. The Council of the State, being desirous of having his picture in full length, requested his sitting for that purpose which he politely complied with, and a striking likeness was taken by Mr Peale of this city.

The painting was greatly admired as representing the leader with all the dignity and strength of character which he possessed. M. Gérard ordered a replica to take to the king of France, and Don Juan sent five copies to foreign courts. There were other orders for replicas. At thirty guineas each they were a welcome source of income to Peale after the interruption to his painting career by the war. In this painting he shows Washington leaning on a cannon, with captured battle flags at his feet. The blue field with thirteen white stars of the new American flag appears behind the head of a charger, which is just back of the general. In the far distance is Nassau Hall, and there is a suggestion of the Battle of Princeton in the middle ground. Washington wears the blue-and-buff Continental uniform. The wide, pale-blue ribbon across his breast is the insignia of his rank, which he adopted at Valley Forge in order that the soldiers could recognize the commander in chief. Slight variations appear in the backgrounds of the replicas. Landscapes and figures of soldiers differ, and it is possible that these little figures were painted by James Peale. A mezzotint plate of this portrait was made by Peale, and prints from it sold well. The success of the Washington portrait was gratifying to the artist. His paintings would now be seen in European courts. The saddler's apprentice had come far.

Six months after the original portrait was hung in the council chamber of the State House, vandals entered and mutilated the canvas. The damage was reparable, fortunately. But the savage gesture was proof of animosity toward Peale for his participation in the conflict over the state constitution, which had flamed into renewed inten-

sity. Like a thunderstorm dying off in the distance, the
Revolutionary battle front moved southward from Philadelphia, and although bad news of British victories kept
coming, the Pennsylvanians were too absorbed in their
local political battle to pay much heed.

The fight for and against the state constitution had become complicated with other issues until it took on the
aspects of class war. The wealthy conservatives represented by the Republican Society still clamored for a re-
vision of the constitution and also stood for free enterprise
in business. On the other hand, the Constitutional Society, mouthpiece for the people, held to the existing constitution and advocated control of prices, because essential goods and foodstuffs were in short supply and cruelly
high prices were made higher by the low purchasing value
of Continental paper money. Among all the states faced
with formulating individual systems of state government,
none struggled as long or with as bitter conflict as Pennsylvania. For a time chaos reigned until Congress threatened to
take over control of the state unless the foolish struggle
ceased. The accepted state constitution was put into effect
in February, 1777, but bad feeling between the factions
persisted for years with undimmed violence.

Peale, known as a staunch Constitutionalist, outspoken
in his sympathy for the poorer people who were miserable in their inability to buy needed food and clothing, won
honors which he did not seek. He became president of the
Constitutional Society and was nominated a candidate for
the state legislature. To accept these honors, Peale must
make a sacrifice in favor of his convictions; politically he
was now lined up against old friends like John Dickinson,

Robert Morris, and John Cadwalader, to say nothing of
wealthy patrons in general on whom his livelihood de-
pended. To the radicals Robert Morris had become the
scapegoat for powerful merchants accused of keeping commodity prices sky-high. His valuable service to the city
as a member of the Committee of Safety was ignored. The
fact that the money he had raised early in 1777 saved the
army for Washington was forgotten. What loomed large
now was the arrival of a desperately needed cargo of flour
which came to port in one of his ships, flour that was offered
for sale at enhanced prices. Public indignation rose to
fever heat; yet Morris could not see why he was not entitled to a legitimate profit on transactions in which he
had assumed a large risk. At a turbulent mass meeting, a
committee was appointed to remonstrate with Morris
about high prices. When he refused to appear before the
committee, it seized the cargo of flour and distributed it
to the hungry poor. While Peale was glad to see the needy
supplied, he was fair enough to realize that an injustice
had been done Morris.

Because Peale was known as a tactful man, moderate in
action, he was constantly drawn into situations arising
from the conflict between the haves and the have-nots.
The newspapers frequently published articles against the
constitution, and when it was learned that a violent attack had been written by the journalist Whitehead Hum-
phries, the Constitutionalists gathered around his house
to voice their protests. They found themselves confronted
by a gun muzzle projecting from a window. An excit-
able bystander dashed off to call the militia, while another
ran to fetch Peale to reason with the crowd. When the

slight figure of the artist came hurrying down the street, men in the crowd said, "There's Mr. Peale," and militiamen who had been under his command said, "Here comes Captain Peale." Respect for their kindly officer led the men to listen to him. He pointed out the futility of violence, persuaded the militia to go home, and saw the bystanders disperse. His good sense had averted possible bloodshed.

But the Republican Society raised great hue and cry. Shame to the Constitutionalists for calling the militia to attack a man in his own home! They accused Peale of inciting the disturbance and had him haled into court. There was not a ghost of evidence against him; too many had witnessed his successful peacemaking. He was dismissed, shaken by this injustice. He was still more disturbed when he was assaulted in the street by a bully about twice his size. He fought him off valiantly, injuring his hand in doing so. A Constitutionalist carpenter, hearing of this incident, presented Peale with a heavy cane of seasoned ash, hard as iron, which Peale dubbed "Hercules." Never without it, he beat off an assailant the first day he carried it. At night "Hercules" hung beside his bed. The artist never felt safe, day or night, in those turbulent years.

The militia was inspired with a desire to drive the wives and children of profiteers out of the city, an ignoble action which Peale was able to prevent. But the militia was steamed up to do something, so the men turned their attention to leaders of the Republican Society, determined to wreak vengeance on these important personages. Peale heard of this new plan and dashed to the rendezvous of the men, but this time he exerted his eloquence and wisdom in vain. As he walked sadly away, the militia

started marching around the city, loudly threatening
thirty well-known men, Robert Morris among them. Morris and his friends prudently took refuge in a stoutly built
house belonging to James Wilson. Wilson had been one of
the signers of the Declaration of Independence but had
aroused the animosity of the radicals by acting as defense
counsel for Loyalists accused of treason.

Like a growing snowball, the militia picked up numerous sympathizers as they paraded about. Finally they
formed a large and menacing crowd that surrounded the
Wilson house. The beleaguered nabobs in the house sent
a messenger to ask the City Troop to come to their rescue.
The Light Horse Troop of the City of Philadelphia was an
organization of young aristocrats who were always prominent in city affairs, military and social. As scions of
wealthy families they were unpopular with the militia,
who were drawn from the people.

The unruly, milling crowd heard the crisp clatter of
hoofs on the pavement, and cries arose, "The Horse! The
Horse!" As the Troop appeared, each member was smart
in his uniform of brown with white facings, round black
hat topped with waving bucktail, and a saber at his side.
The crowd quieted down at its arrival, and soon all was
so serene that the Troop could ride back to its mess hall
at dinnertime. No sooner were the troopers gone than a
shutter at the top of the house opened. A one-armed
veteran leaned out and yelled insults at the militia, waving a pistol in his remaining hand. That was too much
for the militiamen. They fired, and their shots were returned from within the house.

Peale heard the gunfire and started to leave his house

to go to the scene of action. Mrs. Peale, Peggy Durgan, and Rachel, however, clung to him with such combined strength that struggle as he did, raging and fuming, he could not free himself. While this domestic tussle was under way, the troopers, a good dinner under their trim belts, returned to the Wilson house. Seeing what had happened, they charged the crowd with drawn sabers. They took a number of the militia prisoners and jailed them in the courthouse. Darkness had fallen and the mob moved away, muttering ominously.

Next morning a crowd made up largely of militiamen stood outside the courthouse. They were vehemently protesting the imprisonment of members of the militia and were in an ugly mood. Peale hurried to the courthouse with a constructive suggestion. He proposed that bail be given for the prisoners so that they could be released until the matter could be reviewed when feeling had cooled down. Friends stepped forward with bail, the men emerged, and the crowd dispersed. There was gratitude toward the man whose sensible solution had prevented further violence.

When state elections took place in October, 1779, the Constitutionalists swept into the legislature in a veritable avalanche, and Peale became a member of that single-chambered body. An honor, yes. But Peale paid a price for his championship of the common people. There were almost no orders for portraits coming to him because of the resentment toward him felt by the wealthy. His legislative work—he was on more than thirty committees during his term of office—left him no time to seek new patrons. For a time his painting career came to a standstill.

Had he wished it, Peale could have played a leading role in politics for years to come, for his personal popularity would have carried him to high governmental positions. But he wanted only to get back to his painting. He felt he had given his share of public service. He was profoundly tired. His nerves were worn by the strain which war, family cares, and political conflicts had put upon his sensitive nature. For months Peale struggled with a mental lethargy that lay upon him like a leaden weight.

His term in the legislature ended late in 1780, and Peale left politics forever, rousing himself to a happy project. The Peales were to have a new home, and in it a cherished dream would be realized.

20

There Are Illuminations

WHEN PEALE purchased the square, two-story-and-attic
brick house on Lombard Street, he looked lovingly at the
deep lot that ran along Third Street to an alley which
bisected the long block. Peale had a plan for the open space
between the house and the servants' brick cottage. The
interior of the house was typical of Philadelphia houses;
it had a basement kitchen, living rooms, and dining room
on the street floor, and bedchambers on the second and
attic floors. There were good fireplaces throughout, a few
of which were fitted with Franklin stoves. The sanitary
conveniences were in the yard, in the accepted style of
the period, and a portable tin tub served for baths. It was
a roomy house, capable of accommodating Peale's ever-
increasing family. The brood had just been augmented by
a son born August 22, 1780. His name, Titian Ramsay,
honored both the painter of the admired "Venus" and the
well-loved brother-in-law. The roster of the household now
read: Charles, Rachel, Mrs. Peale, James Peale, lately
resigned from the militia, Raphaelle aged six, Angelica
five, Rembrandt two, Titian Ramsay, Charlie and Betsey
Polk, Peggy Durgan, and the slaves.

Rachel was contented in the new house, feeling she had a permanent home at last. She was proud of the Turkey carpets in the parlor, bought at a sale of confiscated goods. Carpets were still a rarity, and these gave the room an air of elegance far superior to the usual floor covering of patterned sand. New furniture, too, gleaming in highly polished mahogany, distracted the eye from the veterans of their many moves. The largest street-floor room, dedicated to Peale for his painting room, stood ready to receive the patrons who, alas, did not come; the antagonism toward Peale still persisted. Philosophically he turned to enlarging to life size the sketches of important Revolutionary figures he had made during recent years; for he now had definite plans for a gallery in which to show them. The fine open space along Third Street offered an ideal location, and Peale had drawn up plans for a long, narrow, windowless room to be lighted by skylights. It was the first structure in America to use that form of lighting. Since business had been poor, Peale did not have capital to put into the building of the gallery; but with customary ingenuity, he devised a pay-as-you-go method which he describes in his memoirs:

As he had not spare cash more than was sufficient to purchase the materials, he conceived the idea that by painting miniatures half price he could get full employment. . . . Therefore he made known that he would paint portraits in miniature for 4 guineas each for 4 months. And he then made this proposition to the Carpenters viz; that he would pay their labour every week but if his success in painting did not allow him a sufficiency of Cash to support his family and pay them, they should stop their work until the one should ballance the other.

The scheme was a success; people of modest means welcomed the chance to have their portraits done at cut rates, and Peale economized by slicing his ivory very thin. The building went ahead without a hitch. All the while Peale seized every spare moment for painting the life-size heads for his gallery. There were Washington, the French minister Gérard, Lafayette, and French, German, and Polish officers who had joined the American cause. He also included men of science and leaders in the government. When the building was finished and the gallery walls had been plastered, there were about forty portraits ready to hang, a stupendous feat of industry and concentrated effort. The family looked with pride at the double row of paintings well lighted from above. Raphaelle experimented with the curtains which could be drawn across the skylights when the sun shone too brightly; they moved smoothly and controlled the light efficiently. Political differences of the subjects were ignored; Robert Morris and Tom Paine hung side by side and never said a word about their differing political creeds. After all, both had given invaluable service to their country. All was ready for the public and the *Independent Gazeteer* announced:

We hear that Mr Peale has completed his new exhibition room which is open for the reception and entertainment of all lovers of the fine arts, being ornamented with the portraits of a great number of worthy personages.

Peale had hoped that his retirement from politics would soften the animosity of wealthy Philadelphians, but it was the gallery which brought him back to favor. To make this record of leading Americans and their foreign allies was considered praiseworthy and patriotic, and the changed attitude toward the artist who had made it in the public interest resulted in an increasing number of commissions. Old friends came too; Baron von Steuben asked to be painted and Washington ordered a portrait of Lafayette. Replicas of these were added to the gallery.

James Peale, who had helped his brother with the rush of orders for miniatures at reduced prices, had been building up a reputation for exceptionally skillful work. At thirty-four he was considered a confirmed bachelor, but he surprised his family by marrying Mary Claypoole. She was the daughter of the artist James Claypoole whose work, seen on his first visit to Philadelphia, had inspired Peale to make painting his profession. James and Mary were married in the Lombard Street house. The bride was slender and pretty; her groom squarely built and handsome, his frank, kindly face beaming with happiness. They did not have far to go to their home, only a few doors down Lombard Street, in which the increasingly popular miniature painter had his own painting room. James had developed a characteristic style, painting with glowing color, giving his subjects liveliness of expression which revealed their personality. James Peale was making his place as one of the best miniaturists in the annals of American art.

Philadelphia celebrated the Fourth of July each year with appropriate ceremony, beginning with bell ringing —all celebrations in the city began with the clangor of bells—and ending with an illumination of the streets. Candles placed in the windows of houses and other buildings bathed the town in a soft, golden glow. Woe to the citizen who left a window dark, for rowdies roamed the streets peppering all unlighted windows with rocks. A French schoolteacher in 1781 produced a variant on the simple candlelit window; he took out the sash and replaced it with oiled paper on which a sentimental picture was painted in crude color. With candles behind it, it created a novel effect.

When Peale beheld this innovation, he had his familiar reaction, "I can better that!" and itched for a chance to show his version of this type of display. A magnificent opportunity came at three in the morning of October 24, when Colonel Tench Tilghman, Washington's aide de camp, galloped into Philadelphia, bringing Congress news that Cornwallis and seven thousand British had surrendered to Washington at Yorktown, Virginia. In the brilliant engagement which won this victory, the French General Rochambeau had landed three thousand men to aid the Americans in this decisive defeat of the enemy. Posters, hastily printed as soon as the splendid news became known, appeared in all parts of the city:

ILLUMINATION

COLONEL TILGHMAN, Aid de Camp to his Excellency, General WASHINGTON, having brought official accounts of the SURRENDER of Lord Cornwallis and the garrisons of York and Gloucester, those Citizens who choose to ILLUMINATE on the GLORIOUS OCCASION, will do it this evening at Six, and extinguish their lights at Nine O'clock.

Decorum and harmony are earnestly recommended to every Citizen, and a general discountenance to the least appearance of riot. October 24, 1781.

Peale's moment had come. The Peale establishment was in an uproar; everyone except the baby worked to get the illumination ready by six o'clock. Three window sashes were removed, two downstairs and one on the second floor. When the candles were lighted, pictures of Washington and Rochambeau appeared in the lower windows, surrounded by rays of glory, bearing the legend "Shine Valiant Chiefs!" while the upper space fairly shouted "For Our Allies Huzza! Huzza! Huzza!"

Small wonder that the Peale house was the center of attraction that night; onlookers "so crowded the streets that if a Basket was to be thrown out, it could not meet with a vacancy to get to the ground."

Congress remembered this successful display and commissioned Peale to make a public showing of illuminations in the State House yard in honor of the birth of a son to the king of France. The celebration was held on May 13, 1782. After the usual bell ringing, congratulatory speeches, and joyful musket fire, the State House yard was aglow with transparencies laudatory to the French allies who had come to the aid of the young republic. When the king's birthday came along on July 5, Peale had a fine private display of transparencies in his windows, adding portraits of Louis XVI and Queen Marie Antoinette to those he had shown earlier.

Though the war was not yet ended officially, it had become possible to send letters to London once more. Peale wrote to Edmond Jenings and Benjamin West, bringing them up to date on his experiences during the war, the additions to his family, and the exciting news about his gallery of Revolutionary portraits. An answer came from West in due time asking for sketches of Continental uniforms, for he intended to paint some American historical subjects. West had been an innovator in his painting of the "Death of Wolf" by showing officers and soldiers in breeches and boots. Heretofore classical dress was used in such works; witness Peale's painting of Pitt in toga and sandals.

March 24, 1783, the trim French cutter *Triomphe* sailed up the Delaware, bringing news that Britain had agreed to make peace with the United States. The war was over. The British ceased hostilities on April 11, and the terms of peace were read to the public on April 16 in the State House yard, whereupon the bells rang out and transparencies and illuminations shone in the warm spring night. Philadelphia began to make plans for a prodigious celebration that would follow the ratification of the definitive peace treaty by Congress on January 14, 1784. The day set for the city's celebration was January 22, and the state contributed six hundred pounds for an arch of triumph and illuminated decorations to be designed and executed by the "ingenious Captain Peale." His plans were kept secret, for he wanted to have his creation burst upon the public with stunning surprise, which it did, all too well.

As January 22 neared, a large wooden structure was erected on High Street between Sixth and Seventh Streets. Fifty feet wide and thirty high, it had a wide central arch and two smaller arches at the sides. The back of the framework was covered with sailcloth to keep drafts from the lamps which would illuminate the transparencies on the front. For weeks Peale, James, Charlie Polk, and anyone else who could be pressed into service were at work painting on the glazed paper. The result was a wonderful mélange of symbolism, coats of arms of France and the United States, Washington in the guise of Cincinnatus abandoning his sword for the plowshare, Indians, soldiers, implements of war and peace, the virtues personified, elaborate architectural detail, inscribed with suitable sentiments and mottoes, freely painted in strong colors which would be effective at a distance. The paintings would have to be affixed to the arch on the twenty-second.

The crowning touch was an heroic statue "Peace," perched on the roof of the house next to the arch, with lights hidden in the clouds at her feet. These lights would be the first to be seen. Then the illuminated figure would slowly slide down a wire to the top of the arch, which would be the signal for all lights to go on behind the transparencies and for salvos of rockets placed at various points upon the arch to be set off. It was a superb creation; nothing like it had been seen before.

Until dark Charles and his assistants worked like madmen to get all the paintings in place and the lights ready to be kindled. Artillerymen were stationed on the arch to set off the rockets. Charles, James, Peale's newly acquired French servant, and eight-year-old Raphaelle were within the structure ready to light the lamps and candles. It had snowed the day before, and as dusk fell, sleighs with their silvery bells joined the horsemen parading through the streets in intense anticipation of the great moment. Houses were illuminated. Peale's, splendidly furnished with transparencies, was presided over by Rachel who, disliking crowds, had elected to stay at home. Her son Rembrandt recalled "seeing my angel mother sitting in the middle of the room to watch the numerous candles which formed the illumination."

The great moment arrived. High against the sky "Peace" glowed in golden light. A long "ah!" of delight came from the crowd which had gathered before the arch. Peale's servant stood ready to release the cord which lowered "Peace," while the others prepared to touch off the interior lamps. Suddenly a rocket, set off by an artilleryman who had been celebrating too liberally, flared out with a back-fire of sparks which ignited the inflammable varnished paper of the transparencies. In a second flames swept through the structure, setting off bundles of rockets which shot off in all directions. Sergeant O'Neill of the artillery was killed, and many of the spectators were seriously burned. The labor of weeks was destroyed in a moment.

Peale, on the top platform, seized a rope and lowered himself to a lower stage, but his loose coat, billowing out, caught up a bundle of sizzling rockets. Peale jumped wildly to escape the flames, looking like a blazing comet with the rockets shooting out from under his coat. He struck a jutting beam, breaking several ribs, then fell to the ground. He picked himself up, ran into the nearest house to have his flaming clothes extinguished, then commandeered a sleigh to take him home. He burst into the room where Rachel sat quietly guarding the candles, his face black, his clothes in charred tatters, frantic with the pain of severe burns and broken bones. Half fainting with shock, Rachel put him to bed, and there he stayed for three weeks. James and

Raphaelle came home miraculously unhurt, but the French servant was badly burned. He doused himself with cold water to cool the burns and recovered quickly. But Peale, subjected to more orthodox treatment, was incapacitated for weeks, convincing Peale that cold water was the cure for burns.

The gaunt framework of the arch survived the flash fire, and the disappointed citizens of Philadelphia decided that they could still have an arch of triumph. Subscriptions were being raised to cover the cost, but Peale, chagrined by the accident to the original arch, rashly offered to meet the expense himself. Subscriptions abruptly ceased. Peale thus bore the major cost of recreating the arch, though he could ill afford it.

On May 10, 1784, the sheriff of Philadelphia proclaimed the definitive treaty of peace once more, and the second version of the arch, set up opposite the State House, glowed in soft colors and in absolute quiet when darkness came.

There were no rockets!

21

Portraits and
Motion Pictures

ANOTHER SON was born to the Peales a few days before the
second arch of triumph shone silently upon the warm May
night. His father reached into Flanders by way of Pilkington's *Dictionary* for an artist's name, calling the baby
Rubens. It was Peale's fond hope in giving the children
names of great artists that it might incline them to the
profession of painting. It really seemed as if his hope was
being fulfilled, for now, as he worked in the painting room,
an earnest group of disciples surrounded him. At ten
Raphaelle showed definite talent; Angelica drew skillfully;
nephew Charlie Polk plodded along with excellent intention but lacked talent; and six-year-old Rembrandt, an
eager, serious little worker, had uncommon ability.

Peale, who insisted on a good foundation in drawing,
did not allow his pupils to use color until they had attained
facility in draftsmanship. In anticipation of the great day
when he would be permitted to paint, however, Rembrandt
made himself a fearful and wonderful painting box at the
expense of a smashed finger and a variety of cuts. Peale

had equipped a workshop for the youngsters, encouraging them to follow their creative impulses and providing them with all kinds of materials. He had advanced ideas in child training and believed that children should be allowed to do whatever they wished, guided gently by parental advice. Rachel often came to the door of the painting room to look at the delightful group of artists: Peale, looking much younger than his forty-two years, his face alert and glowing with interest as he paused in his own painting to counsel or criticize the children; Angelica and the boys gravely intent as they worked. She wondered about the future. If the boys were to become professional artists, would their wives lead the same unsettled existence that she had known? She prayed that they might have her compensation—the unswerving love and devotion of a tender husband.

Patrons who now came to Peale profited by his matured style and his increased ability to portray the innate personality of his sitters. It was a time of high accomplishment for the artist, and it would be recognized in three official commissions for portraits of George Washington. The first came to Peale through a curious combination of circumstances. Cornwallis's surrender at Yorktown had virtually ended the fighting, but the war had not been concluded officially. This situation bred unrest and discontent among the idle troops of the Continental Army, whose pay was long in arrears and who saw no reason why they could not return to their homes and take up their own lives once more. Forces stationed near Philadelphia mutinied and marched upon the State House where Congress was in session, threatening violence if they were not paid at once.

Because the states were still unwilling to levy taxes, Congress had no funds available to meet the demand of the soldiers. The ominous murmur of angry voices outside the State House sent chills down congressional spines despite the smothering heat of a Philadelphia summer; for the legislators to ask protection from the city militia, which strongly sympathized with the unfortunate regulars, was useless. A decision to continue the session of Congress elsewhere met with a cordial reception. Nassau Hall in Princeton offered a spacious and dignified meeting place—the college was not using the second floor—and Congress withdrew to the little town. Princeton's limited facilities were crowded unbearably, and prices were sent sky-high. Congress needed quiet surroundings, for there were matters of great importance under consideration: peace terms to end the war, a site for the nation's capital, and the draft of a federal constitution to replace the Articles of Confederation.

Washington, awaiting an end of war, was holding a large force of restless, unpaid Continentals in the Hudson Valley near Newburgh. In August, 1784, he came to Princeton to confer with Congress. On September 24 a committee from the faculty of the College of New Jersey called upon him to ask if he would be willing to sit for a portrait, which could be hung in Nassau Hall. It would occupy the frame left vacant when the painting of George II was destroyed by a cannon ball. Washington, with a humorous resignation expressed in one of his letters, agreed to sit:

I am so hacknied to the touches of the painter's pencil, that I am now altogether at their beck and sit like Patience on a monument whilst they delineate the features of my face. . . . At first

I was impatient at the request and as restive under the operation as a colt is of the saddle. The next time I submitted very reluctantly but with fewer flourishes; now no dray moves more readily to the drill, than I to the painter's chair.

In this case he was in so amiable a mood that he presented fifty guineas to the college in token of his respect for the institution.

Peale was sent for and in October wrote a friend that he had "painted a portrait of Genl. Washington for Prince Town Collidge and was at the Commencement. Much entertained." He was referring to social activities rather than undue merriment at a solemn commencement. In the portrait he shows Washington full length. The general holds a sword in his right hand, while his left rests on his hip. Just behind him is the figure of the dying General Mercer, who was slain by a British bayonet in the forefront of the Battle of Princeton. Nassau Hall appears through the smoke of battle in the distance. It is not one of Peale's happiest compositions; Washington's pose is too relaxed to harmonize with the grim details of battle.

Next the State of Maryland ordered a full-length painting of Washington. To this portrait Peale added Colonel Tench Tilghman, son of James Tilghman, of Chestertown. The artist thought that the Marylanders would be proud to remember that he had carried the news of Yorktown to Congress. He also included Lafayette. Washington is shown in full uniform, his left hand resting on a cannon. Lafayette and Tilghman at his left look down at passing soldiers, one carrying the white flag of France with golden fleur-de-lis and another bearing a regimental banner of red and white stripes with a golden eagle in the blue union. Tilghman has the articles of surrender in his hand.

The third commission came from the Virginia assembly, which had voted funds for a statue of Washington "of finest marble." Because there were no important sculptors in America, Jefferson, who was in Paris as United States ambassador, advised the Virginians to employ the noted French sculptor Houdon, and to see that he had a good painted likeness to work from. In July, 1784, Governor Benjamin Harrison, of Virginia, invited Peale to draw a full-length picture of Washington and to send it "on the first ship sailing to France to the address of the Hon. Mr Jefferson."

In October Peale finished the painting—portraying the familiar pose of Washington leaning on a cannon with a detail of the surrender at Yorktown in the middle ground. Owing to slow and uncertain shipping, Jefferson did not receive the painting until April, 1785. As it turned out, Houdon never used it, for he decided to come to America and do Washington from life. The Peale portrait was hung in the Hotel Langeac, Jefferson's beautiful residence in Paris, where it was made part of a collection of portraits which Jefferson was accumulating for himself.

Commissions of such importance added to Peale's prestige as an artist, and the revenue they brought in enabled him to pay off what he owed on the Lombard Street property. What troubled him now was to find some way of bringing more visitors to the gallery of Revolutionary portraits; the response of the public had disappointed Peale. A letter from Benjamin West suggested a means of attracting the public. He described a remarkable show put on in London by David Garrick's scene painter, de Loutherbourg. West could only guess at the mechanism employed —de Loutherbourg was keeping it secret—for producing illuminated pictures that gave an illusion of motion with striking effects in changing colored lights. This challenged Peale's inventiveness; he was determined to work out a technique for a comparable show. After months of experiment and many trials and many errors, he at last found a way to do it. If the spectacle he was about to offer did not draw crowds to the gallery, nothing would.

Peale added a room to the end of the picture gallery, building a small enclosed stage across the back. The stage had a transparent backdrop across which cloud effects could be drawn and landscapes projected by light from behind. Lights at the sides of the stage cast changing colors upon the scene through silk screens of every hue, and on the stage objects were manipulated like puppets. There were wooden waves that heaved up and down while small water pipes within them spurted spray and overhead pipes produced the wettest of rain. Sound effects from off stage included incidental music by several instruments, and a reader was engaged to chant descriptions of certain scenes. He was soon fired, for he introduced dubious jokes into the script; Peale would not permit anything in questionable taste in the performance.

Now for the public! On May 19, 1785, the *Pennsylvania Packet* carried an announcement:

Mr Peale respectfully informs the public that with great labor and expense he hath prepared a number of perspective views with changeable effects, imitating nature in various movements.

. . . This manner of exhibiting pictures, imitations of choice parts of natural objects, in which motion and change is given, is entirely new, at least in this part of the world and cannot be performed without much costly and complicated machinery.

The crowds came, cramming the little auditorium four times a day. They were delighted to have such novel entertainment, for there were few public amusements available. They paid their admission fees and for two hours sat enthralled. The program, which delighted eye and ear, included a gathering storm, thunder, lightning, and rain, giving way to sunshine and bird song; Market Street at dusk as the windows and the street lamps gradually lighted up. There were a peaceful scene on the Schuylkill River showing a mill wheel turned by real water and a naval battle amidst spray dashed up by the breaking waves. A clergyman said that the spectacle was worth coming four hundred miles to see.

As summer came on, Peale devised air conditioning. He suspended from the ceiling twelve canvas flaps that were waved to and fro by a system of belts and pulleys, giving a wholly deceptive illusion of coolness.

The entire Peale household was employed in producing the show, but even so, the moving pictures were costly. Peale wrote Bordley that the admissions did no more than "supply the family with market money." And though agog at the wonders of motion pictures, the audiences showed small interest in the gallery of portraits. There was a physical reason for this; despite the undisputed historical value of the collection, rows of paintings, all of the same size, all heads of men, were monotonous to look at. The casual visitor lacked the ability to appreciate the remarkable variety in characterization which Peale, with his insight into personality, had shown.

The performances encroached on Peale's time to the sad detriment of his painting. He cut out one showing a day and had a barrel organ made to supply the music, freeing the family instrumentalists for other tasks, but the show still took up too much time. The problem solved itself as public interest tapered off, and soon performances were given by appointment only to groups of visitors. Peale could get back to his brushes again.

However a new idea was germinating in Peale's busy brain, activated by the opening of a so-called "American Museum" by the Swiss artist du Simitiére, now a resident in Philadelphia. The museum displayed a collection of snakes, insects, coins, Indian artifacts, and his drawings of various celebrities. One day David Rittenhouse, in conversation with Peale, spoke of this exhibition. He suggested that Charles might well show natural history specimens in his portrait gallery, making it a museum which would have great educative value for the visitors. To idealistic Peale it was an attractive idea, and he trotted over to Dr. Franklin's house to ask his opinion of it. Franklin applauded the possibility of "making the gallery a repository of natural curiosities," and brother-in-law Ramsay saw rosy financial prospects in the intake of admission fees.

A further impetus toward natural history came when a Dr. Brown brought some gigantic bones to Peale, requesting him to make drawings of them. Discovered in the course of some excavations, the tremendous relics had roused the wildest speculations as to their origin, the favorite theory being that they were remains of giants men-

tioned in the Bible. Peale measured the leg bones carefully, and a mathematical reconstruction of a skeleton
based on those figures proved that the giants would have
been seventy-five feet tall, which is large even for Biblical
times.

Contact with these wonders whetted Peale's appetite
for collecting other natural curiosities, but he realized that
he must first equip himself with scientific knowledge about
such matters. He always deplored the inadequacy of his
education, but his keen intellectual curiosity led him to
fill in the gaps through intensive reading. He now read
everything on the subject of natural history that he could
lay his hands on. General interest in the subject had only
recently been awakened through the works of the great
Swedish naturalist Linnaeus, who had scientifically named
and classified plant and animal life. Armed with these books
by Linnaeus, Peale applied himself to mastering his system of classification.

For the time being the museum had to remain a goal
of the future, for Peale wrote to West, "I now find it necessary to travel to get sufficient business in the portrait line
to maintain my family which is not small." Indeed it was
growing, for another daughter was born in 1786. After
careful scanning of the pages of Pilkington, she was called
Sophonisba Anguisciola, the musical name of an Italian
noblewoman accomplished in painting.

Peale had two objects in mind when he started on a tour
in Maryland and Virginia—painting portraits and collecting exhibits for his museum. Wherever he went, he broad-
cast his desire for curiosities, getting a stuffed bird here
and a Chinese sword there, receiving a case of butterflies

or a rattlesnake skin. It became evident that, if he was to get scientifically valuable specimens of animal life, he must collect them himself and learn how to preserve them. He was thankful that his wartime practice had made him a good shot; it would be useful in getting specimens. He gathered up all the information he could find on taxidermy —there was little available—and, on his occasional returns to Philadelphia, experimented in methods of preserving the material he had collected. When she died, Franklin donated the body of a fine Persian cat he had brought from Paris, and Peale tackled the problem of stuffing the skin with such poor sucess that the cat had to be hastily interred in the back yard. Gradually his technique improved, for as ever he refused to be discouraged by failures and difficulties and doggedly tried again.

When he traveled, his light carriage was stocked with materials for taxidermy as well as painting equipment, for he shot specimens he saw in the woods and fields and prepared the skins on the spot. Back home, the box containing the skins was unpacked and work on mounting them begun at once, but no sooner were they successfully mounted than they fell prey to moths. Peale doused the skins in turpentine to kill the moths only to ruin fur and feathers, which became a sticky mess. After two years of discouraging failures, Peale finally hit on a solution of arsenic which was a good preservative—so much so that some of his specimens are in good condition today—among them pheasants that Lafayette sent as a gift to Washington. The arsenic solution was fine for specimens but hard on the naturalist. Inhaling the dust had a bad effect on his health, and his hands became so sore from the solution that a light fever would be induced. But he did not count the cost as long as he was getting good results from the processing.

As Peale became more and more absorbed in scientific pursuits, he had the honor of being elected to the American Philosophical Society, which in 1743 had been founded by Benjamin Franklin as "A Proposal for Promoting Useful Knowledge among the British Plantations." Although it was called the first scientific society in the world, the New World, at least, was not quite ready for it and the organization languished until 1768, when it came to life again. The first scientific paper read before the society was an explanation of the mechanism of Rittenhouse's orrery. At a later meeting Rittenhouse reported his observations on the transit of Venus across the sun, data which was of great importance in establishing the distance between earth and sun. The Philosophical Society was dedicated to a wide range of interest—science, medicine, geography, mechanics, commerce, and American inventions. Dr. Franklin was president, and Peale thought he had provided the society with a most agreeable meeting place in the brick wing he had added to his house on Market Street. The meeting room was on the ground floor with Franklin's fine library in the room above, one of the largest and best private libraries in America. Peale admired an invention of the doctor which he called his "long arm," a mechanical device for lifting down books from the top shelves and returning them. His big armchair, on rockers, had a fan above it which could be kept in motion by a slight movement of his foot as Franklin sat reading, keeping off flies and cooling the air.

Peale found the members of the Philosophical Society

thoroughly congenial and contacts with them stimulating and intellectually enriching. It was gratifying to find in the society not only sympathetic interest in his museum project but also valuable counsel about its establishment. Peale was encouraged to write to European scientists, asking for gifts to the museum of European wild life specimens, a correspondence which was to bring him years of pleasant interchange of information and exhibits.

Getting the museum ready for the public was a gigantic task, and though the members of the family helped to the best of their ability, Peale had to work all day and well into the night for weeks. He was so numb with fatigue when he got to bed that he slept right through a burglary one night. Thieves entered the larder, helped themselves to food that struck their fancy, consumed what little alcohol there was, and made off with the Peales' modest store of silver plate. Charles was mortified to have failed in protecting his home. Had he wakened, "Hercules" would have gone into action with good effect.

The exhibits arranged along the walls of the painting gallery were now in good order, and it was time to launch the museum. Philadelphia was about to be invited to see the wonders within its walls.

22

Peale's Museum

On July 18, 1786, the *Pennsylvania Packet* carried an important notice:

> Mr Peale ever desirous to please and entertain the public will make part of his House a Repository for Natural Curiosities —the Public he hopes will be gratified by the sight of many of the Wonderful Works of Nature which are now closeted and but seldom seen. The several articles will be classed and arranged according to their several species and for the greater ease of the Curious, on each piece will be inscribed the place from whence it came and the name of the Donor, unless forbid.

The wall between the auditorium and the gallery had been removed, making a room seventy-seven feet long. The arrangement of the exhibits was described by a visitor, Reverend Manassah Cutler:

> The walls of the room were covered with paintings. . . . One particular part is assigned to portraits of principal American characters who appeared on stage during the late Revolution. . . . I fancied myself introduced to all the General Officers that had been in the field during the war for I think he had every one, and to most of the members of Congress and other distinguished characters. . . . Under a small gallery curiosities are arranged in a most remarkable manner. There was a mound of earth, considerably raised and covered with green turf, from

which a number of small trees branched out. On the declivity was a small thicket and just below it an artificial pond. . . . On the pond was a beach on which was exhibited a fine assortment of shells, turtles, frogs lizards etc. In the pond was a collection of fish, waterfowl, such as geese, ducks, cranes, etc., all having the appearance of life for their skins are admirably preserved. On the mound were such birds as commonly walk the earth.

Peale's imagination and feeling for beauty had created a method of display which antedated modern habitat groups by at least a hundred years, for as the collections grew in number, he showed the animals against painted backgrounds reproducing their natural surroundings and introduced specimens of grasses, moss, and other growths proper to the locale. He sculpted the form of the animal in wood, accurately proportioned, in a lifelike pose and fitted the skin over the wooden base, which gave results far superior to the stuffed skins of ordinary taxidermy. As a creative achievement, his presentation of specimens ranks with his painting, for it was the free invention of an active, searching mind, always striving to improve existing techniques or to replace them with devices original with himself. His eagerness to learn something new, to increase his intellectual range, is reflected in the educative direction given to his museum; he aimed to endow his visitors with knowledge about the wonderful world of natural history. To that end he labeled the exhibits with care, basing his classification and nomenclature on the best authorities on the subject.

During the year 1787 he temporarily replaced his collection of portraits with 130 paintings by Italian artists which had been sent on consignment to certain affluent Philadelphians who were accumulating private collections of European art. The paintings were in poor condition after their long sea voyage, but Peale retouched and revarnished those which needed attention before exhibiting them. Rembrandt was enraptured with these paintings and raced home from school each day to join his father in leafing over pages of Pilkington's *Dictionary* to learn something about the artists represented.

However, as Peale wrote in his memoirs, "He could not have persevered in the labour [of building up the museum collection] when attended with expense if he had not possessed talents for Portrait painting which enabled him to maintain a sufficiency to support, with economy, his encreasing family." In short, it was necessary to be off on a painting trip again, and since he had several commissions in Annapolis, he took Rachel with him—Rachel's heart was always partly in that beloved place. Fourteen-year-old Raphaelle went along, too, to help his father in collecting specimens, and his mother was proud to show her tall, talented boy to her old friends. In between sittings Peale mounted the State House tower to make "8 Birdseye views of the adjacent country and City which will compleat a circular view." His aim was to make a large panoramic engraving from these sketches.

Rachel found the freedom from household cares most refreshing and looked prettier than ever, her dark hair loosely bound with a ribbon, her dark eyes bright with happiness. Peale was sure that never, despite all the charming ladies he had painted, had he seen as perfect an oval as the line of his wife's face. Rachel and the boy went home ahead of Peale, who had a number of orders to fill

along the way; his return was made even slower by the
vagaries of his balky horse. When the animal refused to
budge, Peale relaxed in the saddle, took a book—most certainly on natural history—out of his pocket and read im-
perturbably. The horse found this policy of nonresistance
extremely boring and finally moved along of his own accord. Charles stopped to see the Ramsays who were back
in Charlestown; it proved to be the last time he saw his
lovely sister Margaret Jane, for she died soon afterward.

When Peale returned to Philadelphia, the city was rife
with plans. The federal Constitution had been approved
by Congress, then meeting in New York after one session
in Annapolis, and was now awaiting ratification by the
individual states. The city fathers decided to stage a celebration as soon as the needed majority of nine states had
accepted the instrument, and when the ninth state came in
on June 21, chose July 4 as the day on which the anniversary
of the Declaration of Independence and the ratification of
the new Constitution would be feted at the same time. A
colossal parade was planned, and Peale walked up and
down the streets with the committee which was choosing a
line of march, settling on a central route three-miles long.
An acquaintance, a butcher, asked Peale's help in beautify-
ing the victualers' section of the parade, and Peale noted
that he "was called up early to decorate the Beeves which
the butchers carried in the procession. I was doubly induced to assist in this labour as they had agreed to give
these pieces to the poor." He left no description of the nature of the decoration, but having performed this friendly
deed, he joined James and the older children at a vantage
point along the line of march.

The chimes of Christ Church had been rung at dawn with every lively tune as cannon thundered a salute of thirteen guns. At half past nine the procession got under way and was three hours in passing. There were military units, bands, groups of city officials, and representatives of the professions and trades who carried colorful banners depicting their occupations. There were also many elaborate floats, some with complete workshops in which artisans were plying their trades. The blacksmiths' float with a chimney and glowing fire in the forge was a huge success. Peale watched for the victualers who had some "Beeves" on the hoof immediately followed by white-aproned cleavers. Their fate pursued them, for the "Beeves" would be slaughtered, hides and tallow sold to buy bread for the poor, and the meat distributed to the needy.

The march terminated at Union Green where, after speeches, a fine cold collation was served to all participants in the federal parade. Only beer, ale, and cider were served with the food, which guaranteed an orderly climax to the celebration. The trades, which had been having hard going in the postwar period, were gratified by the prominence they had been given in the celebration. It bolstered their morale and made the citizens as a whole proud of their city. Philadelphia certainly knew how to stage good celebrations.

In the autumn of 1788 the Peale's eleventh child was born. After careful conning of Pilkington, she was named Rosalba Carriera for an Italian "paintress." Rachel never recovered her strength after the baby's birth and gradually sank into the state known as "a decline," in other words, tuberculosis. Charles could hardly bear to leave her when he and Raphaelle had to start on a long tour southward, spending most of the winter in Annapolis and Baltimore. Raphaelle was becoming a fair painter of portraits. He set aside time when he could to paint common objects like fruits, vegetables and pottery, joining the few American artists who were painting still lifes, a field in which he achieved his finest work.

By April, 1789, Peale was back home devising plans for a welcoming ceremony for the newly elected President of the United States; George Washington would pass through Philadelphia on his way from Mount Vernon to New York, where he would be inaugurated. Washington was taken by surprise when he was met at the Pennsylvania border by the smartly accoutered City Troop, sent to act as a guard of honor into the city. As he neared Philadelphia, he was asked to leave his traveling coach and mount a handsome charger provided for him. He crossed the Schuylkill at Gray's ferry on the same bridge of boats over which he led his troops toward the battle of the Brandywine, but he hardly recognized the bridge which was banked in greens and decorated with flags. The river was crowded with gayly adorned pleasure boats filled with people in their Sunday best. There was an arch of green at the end of the bridge from which a crown of laurel hung suspended, held by a cord in the hand of Angelica Peale, who looked angelic in her white gown, her dark hair bound by fillets of laurel. When the general reached the arch, Angelica loosed the cord, and by a miracle, the wreath landed on Washington's brow amid the wild cheers of the bystanders. Legend has it that the general kissed the pretty maiden, but because he disliked demonstrations in his honor, he must have been more inclined to bite her.

Another painting tour lay ahead, and it nearly broke Peale's heart to leave his dear wife, frail and weak, just a shadow of herself with hollow cheeks crimson with fever. There were a number of commissions to fill and gaps in his collections which should be bridged. It was comforting to spend some time with Bordley at his estate on the Eastern Shore, where he was making valuable agricultural experiments and building up a self-sustaining plantation colony. Charles listened to Bordley's plans with intelligent interest, storing up information to share with another dear friend, Thomas Jefferson, a passionate agriculturalist whose official duties at present kept him from putting his theories into practice at his estate Monticello. Peale painted a delightful portrait of Bordley during this visit and put all the watches and clocks on the plantation in running order.

Not until January, 1790, was Peale able to get back to Philadelphia, but he returned with a well-filled purse and sixty fine bird specimens for the museum. He found Rachel failing rapidly, racked with coughing, and trying to direct the household activities, for both Mrs. Peale and Peggy Durgan were too old to carry much responsibility. Charles eased her frail shoulders of all burdens, but not even his tenderest care could arrest the progress of the disease. In April, after touching farewells to her seven living children in which she bade them be dutiful to their father and lead worthy lives, she slipped out of life as gently and as sweetly as she had lived. Charles could not let her go; terrified that she might be buried alive, he postponed interment for

days. When at last she was laid to rest in St. Peter's churchyard, he refused to have the bell tolled; he thought the
doleful sound would be too depressing to the sick who
would hear it. Nor would he permit the family to wear
mourning; they must set an example to poorer people, who
ought not incur the heavy expense of mourning outfits when
death came to their relatives.

On the day Rachel was buried, Peale's wise and beloved friend Benjamin Franklin died. As the year wore on,
other sorrows came to Peale. Peggy Durgan went to lie
beside Rachel in the churchyard, and then little Rosalba's
brief life was over.

The pressing responsibilities of his life allowed Peale
no time to indulge in sorrow. His grief for Rachel was deep
and in his heart he never ceased to mourn her, but with
the honest realism and singleness of purpose so characteristic in him, he faced the necessity of marrying again and
soon. His children must have proper supervision and care;
his mother at eighty-one could not cope with that troop
of bright, talented, and unrestrained youngsters. Orders
to fill made a painting trip imperative. When he took the
road southward, he had three objectives: painting portraits, collecting for the museum, and finding a wife. He
hired a housekeeper; Betsey Polk and Angelica were
charged with the care of the younger children; James and
Mary promised to keep a watchful eye on the household;
and Peale felt that he could leave. A one-horse carriage
was ready on Lombard Street, designed to carry paints,
canvas, stretchers, sacks for game, guns, and preservative
materials, as well as boxes in which to pack the processed
specimens of wild life. Raphaelle, constantly becoming

more useful as an assistant, was to go with his father, and they now checked over their personal baggage. Raphaelle had six plain shirts, four cravats, and three pairs of striped and mottled stockings. His father, with courting in view, took four new shirts, four old ones, nine stocks, two neckerchiefs, three pairs of silk stockings and several pairs of spotted cotton, and brown thread.

Peale hated to leave that little group. Betsey and Angelica looked somewhat fearful of their responsibility; Rembrandt at twelve was quite resentful at being left behind; Titian Ramsay, a manly boy of ten years, stood with little Rubens, gay four-year-old Sophonisba, and their grandmother who was leaning on her cane. He managed a cheerful good-by. Then Raphaelle touched a whip to the horse, and they rattled briskly off toward the South.

23

A Summer Romance

WHAT WERE the assets which Peale, the potential wooer, had to offer a lady? At fifty he was as slim and supple as he had been in youth; his blue eyes were as alert as ever in his fine-featured, intelligent countenance; his brown hair was receding only slightly on the high forehead. He had a wide reputation as one of the foremost American painters; his museum and gallery of Revolutionary portraits were highly rated as worthy projects; he was popular with a distinguished acquaintance; and he ranked as one of the outstanding citizens of Philadelphia. In the other pan of the balance, he was somewhat deaf and had six children, but surely those handsome youngsters, full of promise, could not be counted a liability—any woman should be proud to be a mother to them.

At the moment, as they drove along the country roads, the suitor was feeling far from well. He had been working so constantly with arsenic solution and dust that his health had been affected. The roadside thickets were full of blackberry canes, loaded with luscious ripe berries which the travelers stopped to gather quite frequently during the day. Having eaten quantities of the berries, Peale

soon began to feel better. From that time onward he ex-
tolled the medicinal properties of ripe blackberries.

Wherever they stopped to paint or collect museum material, Peale had his eye out for a suitable spouse. In a
household in Maryland he met a charming widow who
seemed to have all the qualifications he had in mind.
When he delicately broached the subject, he found the
lady was a snob who considered a painter socially inferior.
Later, while painting a lovely young girl whose face had
no animation, Peale said, "Now look at me as if you were
trying to captivate me." She succeeded so well that he felt
his heart beating faster, but he steeled himself against
her enticements. She was far too young to make a sensible
mother to his brood. The portrait, however, benefited by
the livelier expression.

Peale and Raphaelle stopped at Chestertown to see
James Tilghman, now eighty-five, and there met a most
attractive young relative of the old gentleman. But the
old political enmity remained. When Tilghman saw that
Peale had intentions of wooing fair Polly, he made it evident that his suit would not be favored. In addition he
spread unpleasant rumors, completely unfounded, about
the artist. When they turned back to Philadelphia, the
carriage was laden with valuable specimens. Charles had
had no luck in finding a wife, but he had acquired a stunning "curiosity"—a live cow with five legs, six feet, and
two tails. How her six feet were distributed among five
legs remains a provocative mystery, but at least her milk-
producing machinery was free of spare parts. She supplied
the household with milk, fascinated the public, and was
rapturously received by the children as an addition to the

zoo which they maintained in the yard outside the museum. Their father encouraged their love of animals and instilled in them a sense of responsibility for their care.

When he could spare the time and often when he could not, Peale enjoyed talking with visitors in the museum— sending them away better informed about natural history —for his educative zeal never flagged. One day he encountered friends who brought a visitor from New York with them, Miss Elizabeth De Peyster. Following a guided tour of the collection, the party sat down for a chat and, all loving music, for a little singing. Peale was charmed with Miss De Peyster's voice; she carried her part in "Hush Every Breeze" with musicianly skill. In a confidential tone Peale said to her host, "So sweet a voice bespeaks a harmonious mind." The lady was plump, possessed a serious motherly air, was twenty-six years of age, and talked volubly. She seemed drawn to Peale, and he was strongly attracted to her, grasping at an invitation to call upon her with enthusiasm. On his first visit Charles said sadly that it was difficult to find a good mother for his six children.

"My father had a family of children," remarked Miss De Peyster, "but he found a second wife without any trouble." These encouraging words led Peale to believe that he might pay his court to the lady with some success. He was quite right; it was not long before she slipped a gold ring on his finger to plight their troth and wrote to her father in New York. De Peyster was a wealthy Dutch merchant, rigidly conventional, from whom consent to their marriage must be obtained. While they waited for an answer to this important missive, Charles painted a portrait of Betsy with whom he was now sincerely in love.

Sorrow broke into the sweet course of romance when Mrs. Peale, long ailing, died at the age of eighty-two. When Charles returned home after the funeral, he stood for a long time looking at his painting of their happy family group, so lovingly united in life. Now of them all only he and James remained. His eyes lingered on Rachel's dear, dark head; he felt certain that she would be glad he had found someone to be a second mother to her children.

There was still no letter from New York, and the lovers were growing impatient. They decided to go to New York with a party of friends headed in that direction, taking sixteen-year-old Angelica along as a chaperone, quite unaware that they passed the parental letter on the way. The journey was a spring idyl for Peale "with the dear object of my affections still heightening the pleasure with her pleasing converse, her sweet attentions, her melodious voice in enchanting songs. I had nothing to interrupt my happiness but a little dust."

He was well covered with dust when they drew up to the massive De Peyster mansion in New York. Despite his travel-stained appearance, Mr. De Peyster received him cordially, told them he had consented to the marriage, whereat all concerned plunged into a joyous welter of sentiments appropriate to the happy moment. Angelica and Charles were invited to be house guests, and Peale lost no time in commencing a miniature of his father-in-law to give to his sweet Betsy. There were sightseeing tours in New York, which seemed superior to Philadelphia in some respects, family dinner parties, and a picnic held on the green shores of the Hudson River. Betsy and Charles withdrew from the others for a while to enjoy the beauty of the stately river, "while we had our eyes feasted with this pleasing perspective view of great distances . . . Betsy looked charming and delighted my ears with her melodious voice in several songs. We strummed the guitar and talked of love." And yet the lover was sufficiently detached to note what fine wood there was in a raft of logs being towed down the river.

May 30, 1791, Elizabeth De Peyster and Charles Willson Peale were quietly married in her home, and immediately afterward set off for Philadelphia for a visit with the children. Peale's heart swelled with happiness when he saw that the youngsters responded nicely to Betsy's motherly demeanor. A great weight slipped from his mind. Now his family would know a mother's love again, and his household would be directed by a firm and efficient hand, for Betsy had had good Dutch upbringing in the domestic arts.

The honeymoon began with a painting tour in the South. They paused to visit old friends and let them know the new Mrs. Peale. At Bordley's plantation they were promised the traditional flitch of bacon if they lived the first year of their marriage without a quarrel. Poor Betsy encountered a malarial mosquito and was miserably ill throughout most of the trip.

Still white and shaky when they returned home, she took up her duties as a mother to the children. Except for Betsey Polk, there were only Peales in the house now. Charlie Polk had set himself up as a portrait painter in Baltimore, producing uninspired work with great earnestness. Betsy's task was not an easy one; she had been brought up in the disciplined orderliness of a Dutch house-

hold and had been taught that anything less than a spotless kitchen was positively sinful. In the Lombard Street
house the kitchen was frequently used as a laboratory for
preparing specimens; there were odd smells and unpleasant messes. The children's pets had the run of the house.
The place swarmed with young fry, for James Peale had
two little girls and a boy who were in and out every day
and Betsy's sister Mrs. Flagg often came with her own
children and two Indian youngsters she was bringing up
"in a civilized way." It was a fearful strain on the bride,
but she was a good soul and tried to bear her trials with
Christian resignation.

The older boys were engaged in mature pursuits. Rembrandt at thirteen had left school to devote himself exclu-
sively to painting and now at fourteen had a definite professional status. Raphaelle's reputation as a painter was
good. Titian's bent was for natural history; he was especially useful in the museum, though all the boys had become skillful in their father's method of taxidermy. Peale
turned over many commissions to his sons; he had already
given James all the orders for miniatures.

Income from admissions to the museum was substan-
tial. Peale now felt he could devote the major part of his
time to the collections, now enriched by contributions from
abroad sent in exchange for American rarities and constantly enlarged by the material which Peale and the boys
collected. The bird groups were becoming more complete and would eventually run into thousands of specimens, antedating the collections of American birds made
by the ornithologists Alexander Wilson and John James
Audubon. Among the rare exhibits were some platypuses

from Australia supplied by a British naturalist. These odd duck-billed, egg-laying mammals attracted much attention; Peale wished he could see one alive. He was beginning to feel that the museum was too large and important to be solely in his hands and in January, 1792, advertised in the *American Daily Advertiser* for voluntary assistance from scientifically inclined men. The result was a board of visitors made up largely of his Philosophical Society friends—among them were Bordley, Robert Morris, Rittenhouse, and Jefferson—but the weight of responsibility still rested on Peale's slender shoulders.

He found healthful relaxation that winter when the Delaware froze over and all Philadelphia went skating; the ice cracked under the weight of thousands of skaters, yet held up. There were a few conspicuously graceful skaters. Among them was Charles Willson Peale, skimming swiftly on blades curved back gracefully at the front which looked to one observer "as if they had been sent from Germany for Peale's Museum." All the Peales were taught the art of skating, for Peale believed that mild outdoor exercise was essential to good health. He guided the course of Sophonisba, safely navigating on double blades, while Raphaelle pushed Betsy around on a chair sled.

In September, 1792, a son was born to Betsy and Peale. He was named Van Dyke in recognition of his mother's Dutch ancestry, the last artist's name to be bestowed on a Peale baby. Van Dyke was initiated into collecting expeditions at an early age, for the next summer Peale took Betsy and the baby when he and Titian traveled by boat to get specimens of shore and ocean birds for the museum. Science was slightly hampered by the presence of a wife and infant, but some excellent material was secured, which would complete important bird groups. Always, when collecting, mosses, twigs, and grasses were gathered to make authentic habitat backgrounds—again long anticipating modern procedures.

As their little sailing vessel approached Philadelphia, they met an uncommon number of small craft fleeing the city. They were filled to the gunwales with people who cried out to them as they passed, "Stay away! There is plague in the city. Stay away!" Stay away when they had no idea what might have happened to the rest of the family! They made more speed, rowing when the wind slackened, and as they neared the shore, the mournful tolling of church bells spoke of death. A pall of heavy, humid heat was intensified by smoke from myriad bonfires, which were kept burning in a effort to purify the air. Philadelphia was mortally stricken with an epidemic of yellow fever, brought by a visitor from the West Indies.

When they landed, Peale carried the baby and with Betsy clinging to his arm hurried home, leaving Titian to struggle with the baggage. Betsy screamed when she saw a corpse lying on a doorstep and tried to cover her face when they passed a burial cart heaped high with roughly fashioned coffins. It was a great relief to find the Lombard Street household in perfect health, and Peale at once sequestered the family, allowing no one to leave the house. He ordered vinegar sprinkled over clothes and furniture to kill infection, and to clear the air, he and Titian fired blank cartridges in the rooms at intervals.

The humid heat never lifted; not a breeze stirred. The hospitals were dreadfully overcrowded, and the sick fell dead in the streets. The doctors were divided in their method of treating the tropical disease. Some purged and bled their patients to excess; others administered quinine; but under either treatment the victims died with equal rapidity and the overworked doctors succumbed as well. The bells tolled on until the mayor ordered them silenced; the depressing dingdong day and night was too disheartening to the living.

Peale's precautions did not prevent Betsy from contracting the disease. The family physician, Dr. Hutchinson, died of the plague, and rather than risk the ministrations of a stranger, Peale cared for his wife, relying on common sense in his treatment. Only he and Angelica entered the sickroom. Betsy was given frequent, large draughts of barley water to drink and a little laudanum when she was in pain. Her bedding was occasionally moistened with vinegar, and the windows were opened from time to time to freshen the air. Thanks to his quarantine, no one else in the family contracted yellow fever; a servant who lived outside the house was the only exception. One evening, worn out with nursing his desperately sick wife, Peale thought he was coming down with the disease. To supply his body with fuel for the fever to feed on, he ate a large meal of bread and molasses and washed it down with a mug of gin and water. The symptoms vanished at once.

News of the death of the family physician had been received with unabashed glee by ten-year-old Rubens. Always a sickly child, he had been subjected by the doctor to months of nauseous dosage. Now he galloped blithely to the shelf where his medicines were kept, cast them into the kitchen fire, and in his exuberance ran out into the forbidden out-of-doors, seized a watering can, and lavishly sprinkled plants which he had been raising. After this wholesome outburst, Rubens's health improved under a regime of his own selection, which met with his father's approval.

As in other things, Peale was ahead of his times in matters of health. He believed in moderation in eating and drinking, mild exercise in the open air, indoor exercise in reading aloud and singing, and the use of vegetable purgatives like flaxseed in place of the devastating drugs then employed. In the days when females from the age of six onward wore rigid, tightly laced stays, he insisted on loose clothing for the members of his household. For those with weak digestions he advocated a number of small meals during the day instead of the staggering repasts then in vogue. He thought it would be advisable for the city to maintain health stations where people could be taught to keep themselves in good condition; they would be better equipped to withstand epidemics.

Some years later Peale embodied these ideas in a pamphlet "An Epistle to a Friend on the Means of Preserving Health," which he distributed to his friends and sold in the museum. He advised cooking vegetables in steam to preserve their nutriment and advised slow and careful chewing. The use of tobacco and spirits, unless well watered, was frowned on. But above all, he considered serenity of mind a means of avoiding casual disease. Benevolence of disposition, love of order, and the "endearing wish of communicating happiness to every animate being that surrounds us, are sweet springs of health that flow in all directions if the passages are kept open." Peale's own goodness and his desire to make others happy should have disseminated good health wherever he went.

At any rate, under his treatment Betsy was making a good recovery. When the first frosts came, the yellow-fever epidemic had died out, having brought death to about five thousand Philadelphians. The horror of that terrible summer lingered long in the memory of those who lived through it, and it is not surprising that for years afterward, as midnight approached, extraperceptive citizens saw a ghostly hearse, heavy with black plumes, drawn by jet-black horses, and driven through the streets by the Devil himself.

24

A Museum
on the March

Dᴜʀɪɴɢ ᴛʜᴇ yellow-fever epidemic, the Peales were obliged
to ask the affluent De Peysters to forward enough money
for the necessities of life. Peale's income dropped to zero;
he could not go out to paint portraits, and the museum had
to be closed until the plague died down. With remarkable ability to make the most of time no matter what was
happening, he devoted this period to improving the museum with the aid of the older boys. They rearranged the
collection of minerals, classified and labeled them more
accurately, and set up the recently acquired aquatic birds
in natural settings. Everything was freshened up for the
reopening of the museum.

Seventeen thousand Philadelphians who had fled during
the epidemic now straggled back, and city life began to
run in normal channels. To draw attention to the museum,
its founder hit on an effective device. He announced publicly that a subscription book for "friends of science" would
be opened, and for a dollar—dollars and cents had been
made the units of national currency in 1791—a "friend"

was entitled to visit the museum at any time in the course of the year. The public responded enthusiastically. Practically everyone of consequence, and many of none, signed the book, with the agreeable result that the museum acquired capital to work with.

Now that Congress had left New York and Philadelphia was once more the seat of government, President Washington often visited the museum to see his friend Peale. He had taken four subscriptions for the year so that his family could enjoy the museum at all times. His Secretary of State, Thomas Jefferson, was deeply interested in natural history and had great respect for Peale's venture. He, too, was a frequent visitor, and he and Charles had long talks about the wonders of nature, common-sense living for good health, progressive education, and music. Music was a close bond, and Jefferson liked to add the notes of his violin when the family sang, Betsy's voice leading them.

Peale, who had a flair for publicity, sent brief articles to the newspapers under noms de plume, describing noteworthy exhibits in the museum collections or advancing an unsound theory about some specimen, which brought indignant letters to the press and sent people flying to the museum to see for themselves, which was just what Peale intended. Writing over his own name, he appealed for gifts of woods native to America, fossils, "birds, beasts, reptiles and insects, alive or dead." Hoping to limit the donations to exhibits needed, he discouraged the odd "curiosities" which the donors deemed worthy of exhibition. One article not written by Peale said of the museum:

There seemed to be a place for everything and everything in its place, decorated and enlivened by appropriate miniature landscape scenery of wood and wild, blended and intermingled with insect, bird or beast, all seeming alive but preserving the stillness and silence of death.

In the domestic circle two weddings had taken place. Betsey Polk had married Septimus Claypoole, a relative of James's wife, and one of his friends, an Irish gentleman by the name of Alexander Robinson, many years her senior, had wed Angelica Kauffmann and taken her to Baltimore to live. Peale was still making occasional painting trips with the heavier emphasis on collecting for the museum. On one visit to Baltimore after Angelica's marriage, he shocked his haughty son-in-law by his wholehearted pursuit of beetles, an interest awakened by Dr. Kirtz, a German minister who specialized in collecting these insects. Peale, looking under bushes, overturning stones, and even seeking specimens under lumps of dung, confessed, "I found so much amusement that several hours passed away before I could think of leaving those bewitching animals." His happy, scientific zest did not appeal to Robinson, who considered the antics of his father-in-law distressingly devoid of dignity. Peale was sad—not for himself—because he foresaw that Angelica would not be allowed to see much of her family in the future.

In 1794 Betsy bore her second son, whose name was a compromise between the mother's objection to "fancy" names and the father's belief in the influence of a name on a child's destiny. This time the influence was exerted in the field of science, for the baby was christened Charles

Linnaeus. Science came out on top, for he was always called Linnaeus.

Peale's wish that the museum be given official recognition and become less of a personal responsibility was now to be partially realized. The Philosophical Society had been granted a tract of land adjoining the State House on which it had erected an attractive, roomy, two-storied brick building, which was known as Philosophical Hall. For the present the society had need of but two rooms for its meetings and those of the College of Medicine plus space for its library of scientific books. From the first, the members had shown sympathetic interest in Peale's Museum. Those who owned material pertinent to his collections had lent it for exhibition. It seemed fitting to the society that Peale's collections and their own should be housed in the unused space in the new hall under the aegis of the Philosophical Society. This was distinguished recognition for Peale, and he gladly accepted the conditions imposed. He could rent the second floor of the hall, but his museum must be used to further education in natural history, which had been Peale's objective from the beginning; Peale and his family should live on the premises; Peale should act as curator of scientific collections belonging to the society and act as librarian.

When a kitchen and household offices were installed in the basement and part of the first floor adapted to living purposes, the Peale family moved in on August 1, 1794. Transplanting the family was a simple matter compared to moving the exhibits. The distance from Third and Lombard to Chestnut and Fifth was only six blocks, and Peale was inspired to make the move count as publicity. He hired a crowd of boys, entrusting one specimen to each. After carrying a precious burden to Philosophical Hall, each boy then ran back to get another, so that the stream of exhibits was uninterrupted for hours. When the first animals came in sight, a shout, "There's a bobcat on Chestnut Street," brought crowds to the sidewalks and work along the line of march was suspended for the day. Questions flew: "What's that long-legged critter?" when a crane came past and "Ain't he got no legs?" when a stuffed seal appeared. When the snakes began to arrive, a bibulous gentleman was hauled out of a tavern, and the look of terror on his face when he saw the lifelike reptiles evoked roars of laughter from the bystanders.

The parade of specimens publicized the museum's change of quarters in a most dramatic manner. The crowds hung about, much edified when the Revolutionary portraits filed past one by one, and there was keen competition in seeing who could recognize the largest number of the subjects. Heavy objects were moved by men with carts. The move, made expeditiously and without accident, provided Philadelphia with fascinating conversation for days and created a widespread desire to visit the museum as soon as it was open to the public in its new home.

A spacious walled yard surrounded the hall and the informal zoo was there installed. The children's collection of animals had been increased by gifts of monkeys and baboons, an eagle, a brown bear from Georgia tugging at his chain, and an elk that wandered about in majestic dignity. In one corner the five-legged cow chewed her cud, switched her two tails, and regarded the scene with soft bovine eyes. The live animals would take their place as museum exhibits when death overtook them, but for the present they were unaware of the immortality for which they were predestined. Moses Williams, the dusky servant who acted as museum attendant, often gave visitors an extra treat by feeding the animals in the zoo; the unfortunate simians were often subjected to foods ill-suited to their digestion.

With the museum and his family solidly established within the red-brick walls of Philosophical Hall, Peale could give his attention to a project which had been germinating in his mind as he gave his children lessons in painting. A school for instruction in all branches of art was sadly needed—there was none in America—and contemporary artists, whose number was growing, deserved a chance to show their work under dignified auspices. A permanent showing of great works of art, open to the public, would do much to develop a taste for fine arts among the American people. Peale had been humiliated by the scorn of French artists, who had come to Philadelphia to escape the Terror in France, and English artists, eager to exploit a promising market for their wares, at the absence of art schools and public galleries in the United States. A cooperative effort by the artists with the financial backing of interested laymen should be able to create an institution which would supply these deficiencies.

In 1791 Peale made an attempt to organize foreign and native artists in such an undertaking, but the committee turned out to be a hornet's nest of antagonisms and disputes. In the ensuing squabbles the project fell apart. Indomitable Peale tried again in 1794 with better success, avoiding the disputatious foreign element, and the Columbianum, or

Association of Artists of Philadelphia, was formed. The dues were ten dollars a year, and membership was open to artists and laymen alike. An art school got under way with classes in the various media, perspective, anatomy, and the chemistry of paints. The latter innovation was proposed by Peale because of his own troubles with fugitive colors and pigments which could not be mixed without danger to permanency. Rembrandt was an avid student in the chemistry class.

All-embracing Philosophical Hall provided a room for the art classes, and a small collection of classical casts was gathered in, including one, borrowed from the English artist Robert Edge Pine, of the "Venus de Medici." Because of her total nudity, "Venus" was not put on display. However, an attested professional artist would be granted permission to use her as a model if he did so in complete solitude.

The school started off auspiciously, the classes including the scions of several wealthy families—Peale envisaged them as future patrons of art. As he saw the students assiduously drawing casts, it seemed a dull and lifeless procedure. They ought to be working from living models. All aglow with this progressive idea, Peale proposed a life class at the next meeting of the Association of Artists. The rich young men walked out of the meeting in a body, sending Peale a written protest:

We whose names are hereunto subscribed, highly disapproving of the inconsistent and indecent motion brought forward at the last meeting of the Association, take the liberty of informing them that we consider ourselves no longer members of that Association.

Disapproval meant nothing to Peale when he had his mind set on something which seemed right to him. He presently announced the first session of a life class with a nude model, having persuaded a husky young baker to pose. Courageous students who sincerely wanted a chance to draw from life were seated at their easels in a room properly warmed for the model, who was disrobing behind a screen. When the moment to step out before the class came, the baker balked, hastily donned his clothes, and departed, loudly denouncing the school as the work of the Devil. Peale could not bear to have this first attempt at a life class fail. Asking the students to wait a moment, he stepped behind the screen and then, clad only in dignity, came out to pose for the class.

That was too much for the prudish Philadelphians who accepted the revealing *decolletage* of their women without a qualm but who could not brook the scandalous, shocking thought of a well-known citizen standing naked before a small class of young men. The indignant ran out of adjectives to adequately describe the outrage. The scandal caused the death of the art school and awakened a prejudice against nude models that took long years to overcome.

Happily Peale's admirable efforts to encourage the growth of interest in painting in Philadelphia met with success. In May, 1795, an exhibition of contemporary art was held for six weeks in the Senate Room of the State House. Admission was twenty-five cents. The public response was heartening, for the large showing was studied with interest, pleasure, and local pride. The name Peale appeared frequently in the list of exhibitors. James sent nine miniatures; Rembrandt five portraits; Raphaelle portraits, still lifes, and studies of fish; while Charles Willson Peale showed eight portraits. One of his paintings, a tall, narrow upright, was set into a doorframe in the room with the intention of fooling the public into believing that the figures were alive. Many stories were told of visitors who were deceived; George Washington is said to have bowed to two sons of his friend Peale. Raphaelle was shown starting up a flight of stairs, palette and maulstick in his hand, looking back into the room, while Titian above him, partly hidden by the doorframe, looks down at his brother. The painting may have been considered a success because it deceived the public by its realism, but what Peale really achieved was what is perhaps his finest painting. The composition is original and felicitous in design; the figure of Raphaelle has vigor and movement admirably contrasted to the static pose of his young brother. The painting is one of the treasures of the Philadelphia Museum of Art.

Another child in the scientific series arrived in 1795, but there was a slight delay in naming him. The minutes of the meeting of the Philosophical Society held February 19, 1796, had this entry:

Mr Peale presented to the Society a young man of four months and four days old, being the first child born in Philosophical Hall, and requested that the Society should give the child a name. On which the Society unanimously agreed that after the founder and late president of the Society, he should be called Franklin.

Peale stood with the baby in his arms, looking down tenderly at the little fellow blinking in the candlelight, while the vote was taken. The presiding officer, Rittenhouse, smiled when he bestowed the name of the great man upon the son of his friend Charles.

There was a wide range of age in the family now, from little Franklin to Raphaelle at twenty. Rembrandt seemed older than his seventeen years, and Titian, fifteen, was a manly assistant to his parent in the museum. Rubens was never strong and had poor vision, which had lately been overcome by wearing spectacles—a rare sight on a child— they were supposed to be the sign of age. But Rubens peered through them quite unconcerned and kept watch over rare plants which he was raising, for he had developed a penchant for botany. Sophonisba was a happy little girl of nine; then came a gap left by the death of Van Dyke in his infancy. Now the line of scientists were coming along, Linnaeus leading.

The atmosphere in the home was stricter now, for Betsy was a strong-willed woman. Her insistence on conventional behavior aroused resentment in the older children and built up lasting bad feeling against her. Betsy did not like to take part in the museum activities, for she considered taking tickets undignified for one of her social status. Peace-loving Peale, accustomed from boyhood to family solidarity and cooperation, found this attitude hard to understand. When the atmosphere grew too tense, Peale would take out the four-octave xylophone he had made— he called it the "sticcado"—and induce Betsy to sing. Her voice was sweet.

From the windows of Philosophical Hall, Peale saw President Washington come each noon to set his watch by the clock on the west wall of the State House. He was a striking figure in black satin breeches and coat, pearl-gray waistcoat, silver buckles on his shoes, and a black tricorn hat on his beautifully powdered hair. "He lends dignity to his office," thought Peale, and he wished that, having painted him so frequently in uniform, he might now paint him in civilian garb.

That wish would soon be realized.

25

George Washington
Is "Peeled"

A VIOLENT, meteoric figure burst upon Philadelphia in 1795. An artist came to paint a full-length portrait of President Washington and remained to become a popular painter of Philadelphians. This was Gilbert Stuart; born in Rhode Island, he was brought up in Newport where, while still a youth, he had made a name for himself as an organist. Furthermore, he showed an uncommon talent for painting and attracted the notice of a visiting Scottish artist, Cosmo Hamilton, who took him to Edinburgh as his apprentice. Shortly afterward Hamilton died, leaving Stuart stranded. In desperation he shipped before the mast in a ship bound for America, an experience so horrible that he could never bear to speak of it.

Newport welcomed him back, and Stuart did well with portraiture. But the pasture across the ocean seemed greener; he borrowed money to go to London. He knew no one in the great city and soon found that an unknown artist could get nowhere without important contacts. He was starving when a stroke of luck brought him a position

as organist in a city church, which assured him of food—
and drink—but did not further his career as an artist.

Stuart finally took the path, well worn by American feet,
to Benjamin West's door. With customary generosity, West
took Stuart under his wing but found he had a prickly
nestling there. The young man drank immoderately, got
into scrapes, played embarrassing practical jokes, and was
wholly unreliable. Talent he had—perhaps genius. His use
of color was free and brilliant, and he composed in color,
never troubling to draw the subject. His paintings had a
sparkle and vivacity which, with West to introduce him,
won the favor of London society. He made a great deal of
money but spent more than he made, which landed him in
debtor's prison at frequent intervals. For a time he lived
and painted in Ireland, then fled to America to escape terrific debts. He settled in New York where he readily built
up an excellent clientele. One of Stuart's assets was his
scintillating conversation, which kept his sitters so animated that his portraits were invested with lively charm.
His bouts of drunkenness became a scandal and his children lived in terror of his brutality, but when he exerted
his charm, he was irresistible—except to Washington.

Stuart had expected to find Washington heroic in appearance and was disappointed at the first sitting to find
that Washington at sixty-three had grown heavy and
paunchy and that his face was slightly distorted by ill-
fitted false teeth. "Not romantic," thought the artist, "but
I will get some expression in that stern face." He launched
a stream of witty anecdotes and gay quips in vain; Washington never smiled, his eyes were dull, and his expression
glum. Obviously he did not like the voluble artist whose

face wore a record of dissipation and who incessantly wielded the largest snuffbox ever seen, having acquired the snuff-taking habit as a child in his father's snuff mill. An unresponsive sitter plus a disillusioned artist added up to a painting which neither liked, a fact which did not keep Stuart from making fifteen replicas at high prices.

Just at this time Rembrandt Peale received a commission for a portrait of the President. Peale, delighted that his son could be numbered among the painters of Washington, arranged for three sittings from seven in the morning to ten. At ten promptly, Washington had his hair dressed and powdered. For the first pose Peale set up his easel near Rembrandt's and talked casually with the President, who enjoyed his good sense and progressive ideas. He had no glum looks for friendly, agreeable Peale.

On the day following, Washington sat again for Stuart and on the next returned to Peale, who had decided to let other artist members of his family profit by this opportunity. James was ready with a fine slice of ivory for a miniature, and besides Charles Willson and Rembrandt, Raphaelle and Titian were ready to sketch the President. Peale and Stuart knew each other without much love lost between them, and Stuart told the story of the family at work with a dash of malice:

I looked in to see how the old gentleman [Peale was fifty-four] was getting along with the picture and I found the general surrounded by the whole family. They were peeling him! As I went away I met Mrs Washington.

"Madam" said I, "the general is in a perilous position."

"How, sir?"

"He is beset, Madam, no less than five at him at once; one aims at his eye, another at his nose, another is busy with his hair, his mouth attacked by a fourth and the fifth has him by the button."

"Peeled" or not, this last portrait of Washington by Charles Willson Peale is full of sober dignity, showing the strength of the fine face, the deep-set blue eyes, graying hair not yet powdered, set off by the black coat and soft, ruffled white jabot at the throat. Peale embodied in this painting his admiration and affection for a great man, while Rembrandt's portrait is loosely brushed, just a head, showing a countenance ravaged by age, seen from the viewpoint of youth, lacking the penetration of his father's portrayal. However, Rembrandt exploited the fact that he had painted Washington from life, advertising himself years later as the only living artist who had had that privilege and profiting by the innumerable replicas he made of this painting.

It is interesting to compare these Peale portraits with the head and shoulders which Stuart painted not long afterward, the so-called "Athenaeum portrait," which has been accepted by America as the true aspect of Washington. A brilliant, idealized painting, it is not veracious by comparison with portraits by Peale, Trumbull, and Houdon.

With Rembrandt well launched on his career as a painter and Stuart usurping the field which had been his for so many years, Peale decided to relinquish painting in favor of his sons. His retirement from portraiture was like the farewell to the stage of certain actors, merely an interruption. Peale could no more stop painting than he could stop breathing. However, for the moment commissions were turned over to the boys so that their father could devote himself to the museum.

Raphaelle was traveling constantly on painting tours, and Peale was gravely concerned about his growing addiction to drink. He was sad that his precepts about moderation in the use of spirits had no effect on his son. He was distressed, too, when Raphaelle and Rembrandt determined to set up a Peale's Museum in Baltimore without any scientific purpose; they merely wanted it as a money-maker. Unable to dissuade them, he contributed duplicate specimens from his collections to their helter-skelter display of unrelated natural history material and copies of portraits. The unsound venture did not last long, though it would be revived more successfully years later. Within the year both boys married against their father's wishes, although Rembrandt's marriage proved to be a happy one. Peale thought that their advertising for portraiture was undignified—Rembrandt's "Death deprives us of our friends, and then we regret having neglected an opportunity of obtaining their likenesses" and Raphaelle's "No Likeness No Pay."

Peale was kept busy at the museum with visitors, foreign and American, who streamed through the nation's capital, which was still Philadelphia. Among the visitors were members of a great congress of Indian tribes from beyond the Great Lakes and the Mississippi. The chiefs wore their handsomest ceremonial dress to honor the seat of government. Peale's Museum was included in all sightseeing tours, and he was enchanted to have these magnificent Americans enter his doors.

One day as he was guiding a group of stalwart redskins through the museum, the chimes at the turnstile sounded merrily as a second party of Indians entered. The two groups of Indians confronted each other. They were members of two tribes that were at war with each other! Although the braves were unarmed, black looks were sharp as arrows. For a moment violence seemed inevitable, but Peale reasoned with the uneasy chiefs. Through an interpreter he begged them to note that this was a chance meeting. They were on a pleasure trip, he reminded them, not the warpath. Why not bury the hatchet? With grunts of assent, the two parties took their separate ways in peace. Three days later, under government auspices, sixty-four chiefs from ten leading tribes, held a powwow in Peale's Museum to sign a nonaggression treaty and seal it with a pipe of peace. Peale laid the success of the occasion to the civilizing effect of natural history and took great pride in having provided the background for the event.

His mind was full of inventions at this time, as always. One device on which he was working was a patent chimney in which metal screens prevented heat from escaping up the flue. Also, remembering the countless fords he had splashed through on his painting trips, he was certain America needed bridges which could be constructed inexpensively, and designed one of ingeniously bent and braced planks. A quarter-size model made for display in the museum demonstrated that its "strength is so great that twelve Indians, all stout men, stood on it together and did it no harm." Indians seemed to have been ready at hand when needed. Peale took out a patent on the construction, the first bridge patent issued in the United States, and published "Essay on Building Wooden Bridges." He was pleased with his "smoke eater," a brick stove in which the smoke was drawn back through the fire to use any remaining combustible elements and then passed through pipes under the floor to the chimney. He installed two in the museum, faced with imitation marble and crowned with a classic urn; they were much admired for beauty and practicality.

Betsy's first daughter arrived in 1796, and if she wanted a conventional name for the child, she did not get it. The name chosen was Sibylla Miriam for the German entomologist Sibylla Merian, who had painted the master plates for her book on insects. The pages of Pilkington were no longer turned in search of names; it was taken from the shelf only to record the date of births or deaths.

Since Betsy had not visited her family for years, Peale took her, little Franklin, and the baby with him to New York in the summer following the baby's birth. They traveled by water, a slow but agreeable mode of transportation. New almshouses were being erected in New York, and Peale hoped to have some of his patent chimneys installed. As soon as they arrived in the city, the De Peysters obtained a hearing for him with the city council, which regarded the device favorably; adoption seemed certain. Time was spent pleasurably painting members of the De Peyster family and sightseeing until a letter came from home saying that yellow fever had broken out again and Titian Ramsay was gravely ill.

Returning by stagecoach, Peale made the trip in one long day and was able to get home to treat Titian as he had treated Betsy. So good were the results that after a week the lad seemed well enough to travel. By easy stages he rode in Peale's light traveling chaise to New York. He had planned a collecting trip around Albany, but that project was not carried out, for the exhausted boy died in New York. This was a shattering blow to Peale, for Titian was his right-hand man at the museum and showed brilliant promise as a naturalist. Despite his grief, his remarkable ability to concentrate on his work enabled him, while on this trip, to complete fourteen oil portraits and five miniatures, to prepare thirty museum specimens, to supervise the construction of six patent chimneys, and to secure an order for forty more. In addition he was paid a fee of five hundred dollars for the privilege of building others within the city. With fine understatement Peale said that he had not been lazy.

Next year another son was born. He was given the name Titian Ramsay, and as he grew to maturity, he seemed to pick up his namesake's work where death had interrupted it, a fact that might interest anyone who believed in the transmigration of souls.

Peale had dreams of a school of natural history as an adjunct to his museum. As a move in that direction, he offered lectures on the subject at Philosophical Hall, again proving himself an innovator by illustrating the lectures with natural history specimens. Because he feared that talk alone would not be diverting enough, three intervals of music were interpolated. They were settings of poems by Rembrandt on "Beauties of Creation," "Dirge," and "Ode on the Death of Titian Peale." The last two must have given a lugubrious tone to the occasion. The lectures were by special subscription, single entrance fee of twenty-five cents or yearly subscription, now raised to five dollars.

Thomas Jefferson, third president of the Philosophical Society, soon to be inaugurated in Washington as third President of the United States, had been greatly interested in finds in Ohio of enormous fossil bones. They were similar to those sketched by Peale many years before. American naturalists were irked by a theory advanced by the French scientist Buffon that something in the American climate kept animals from attaining great size—there were no camels, no elephants living. The bones of what was referred to as the "Great American Incognitum" refuted that notion, and a complete skeleton would be proof positive. The Philosophical Society formed a "bone committee" to secure that proof if possible. Peale, naturally, was a member of the committee. Jefferson's concern with this enterprise provoked a threatening poem:

> *Go wretch, resign the Presidential chair;*
> *Disclose thy secret measure, foul or fair.*
> *Go, search with curious eyes for horned frogs*
> *'Mid the wild wastes of Louisiana bogs,*
> *Or where the Ohio rolls its turbid stream,*
> *Dig for huge bones, thy glory and thy theme.*

Peale, ready to "dig for huge bones," was alert for news of any new finds, and one glorious morning he learned that a considerable deposit had been found on a farm near Newburgh, New York. The sixty-year-old artist-naturalist was as exhilarated as a boy when he set off with Rembrandt, taking the express stage for New York on June 5, 1801. He had with him a bulky piece of baggage. It was a steam cabinet of his own invention, which produced a fine sweat with one pail of water. He wanted to demonstrate its curative properties to an ailing uncle of Betsy. With the cabinet well roped to the top of the stagecoach, the two Peales took their seats and were off in high anticipation of discovery.

26

A Mammoth
Is Exhumed

Arrived in New York, Peale set up his steam cabinet, which soon cured Betsy's uncle of a digestive disorder; made a quick collecting trip to Coney Island for sea birds; secured letters of introduction to Dr. Graham, of Newburgh, a man who had appreciated the importance of the find; and with Rembrandt sailed up the Hudson on the sloop *Priscilla*. It was a glorious June day; the scenery was incomparably beautiful as a fresh breeze sped them along between the majestic Palisades and brought them in the shadow of the blue Catskills to a landing at West Point. There a chaise was hired, and the Peales drove to Newburgh and found Dr. Graham eager to show them the site of the excavation on Marsters's farm and lead them to the granary where a heterogeneous mass of bones was spread out on the floor.

Local physicians had done the digging, but the "habits of the men requiring the use of spirits, it was afforded to them in too great profusion and they quickly became so unruly and impatient that they nearly ruined the skeleton."

Many bones were broken, but so much good material was at hand that the excited Peale could hardly control himself sufficiently to join Rembrandt in making sketches of the bones which were intact.

The pit from which these had been so carelessly dug had filled in with water, which no amount of hand bailing could lessen. The sight would have discouraged anyone other than Charles Willson Peale, whose mind was busily contriving a drainage scheme. The first step was to get permission to excavate, and Peale offered a hundred dollars for the right to dig and two hundred dollars for the bones already unearthed. Peale's glee when this offer was accepted was so evident that Marsters quickly demanded, in addition, a gun for his son and dresses for his wife and daughter. The bones were packed in casks and boxes and sent to Philadelphia so that they could be studied before the excavation was started.

Equipment for drainage had to be obtained. Jefferson promised a navy pump and a large army tent, and the jubilant Society lent Peale five hundred dollars to carry on the work. Back at Newburgh twenty-five men were hired, the army tent was set up to house the workers, and a shed for tools was built. Peale found a skilled wheelwright to construct a drainage device from his design, an endless chain of buckets activated by a huge wooden drum that revolved as someone walked within it.

As the work got under way throngs came to watch. It was not necessary to hire anyone to walk the wheel; there was always a spectator eager to contribute foot power to a great scientific undertaking. The wheel had other uses. One night, as Peale slept in the worker's tent, "the wind

N.E. blowed on his shoulder . . . and when he waked he found so much pain and stiffness that he could not put on his clothes." A workman helped him into his coat, and then he "went to the great wheel and walked in it until he became wet with perspiration. This entirely cured his shoulder."

Spring water in the pit was icy, and it was nasty, sloppy work for the men who were digging. Peale found it necessary to issue grog to the men to keep them at work, but he watered it as much as he dared. Bones were being unearthed. However, as the pit deepened, the walls, weakened by seepage, caved in, necessitating a move to another site. Armed with pointed iron rods, Peale and Rembrandt probed in swampy ground which had been cleared of underbrush by the workmen, quickly learning to distinguish between the feel of bone and that of rock, until they discovered a promising site. The drainage equipment was moved up, and fine new deposits were discovered. So far a lower jaw of the "Incognitum" was missing, and no skull pan had been found. In September, when a complete lower jaw came to light, exultant Peale served undiluted rum to all concerned amid rousing cheers. After five months of work, at the cost of a thousand dollars, Peale was satisfied that he had all the members of the animal. He packed finds from the two sites separately and shipped them to the museum.

Next came the exciting task of assembling a skeleton from the collection of bones laid out on the floor of the hall. Peale had to be guided by his feeling for proportion and his knowledge of animal anatomy, for there was no precedent to follow. The only prehistoric skeleton ever assembled had been found in Argentina and set up in Madrid. Rembrandt and Moses Williams worked with Peale on the giant jigsaw puzzle, receiving floods of advice from fascinated onlookers and helpful criticism from members of the Philosophical Society. In three months the tremendous job was completed. The skeleton—an iron bar holding the vertebrae in place, the rib basket fastened to the spine, and the leg bones cleverly joined with hinges— stood 11 feet high at the shoulder and 9 feet at the hips. It was 15 feet long with curving tusks 11 feet in length. A few lacking details were supplied in papier-mâché.

The Philosophical Society had a private view on Christmas Eve. But Jefferson could not be present; he had been inaugurated in the new capital just a week before. Next day the public was admitted for a special fee of fifty cents; the skeleton was shown in a separate room. To announce the opening, a trumpeter rode through the streets. He was followed by Moses Williams, riding a white horse, who was dressed in Indian garb with a flowing feather headdress to symbolize primitive life—the era of the mammoth, as the great creature was now called. The clarion call brought the public in droves; this was the ninth wonder of the world.

There were enough bones to construct a second skeleton, which Peale planned to send abroad for exhibition. The climate of America not produce large animals? Let them look on this monstrous creature! To publicize the European trip, the second skeleton was set up without the leg bones in the hall. Within the great rib basket a large walnut table was placed, and at the side a patent portable piano, invented for the occasion. In that novel enclosure Rembrandt gave a dinner to thirteen distinguished guests. Many toasts were drunk amid a barrage of puns, much relished by the party; it was a truly newsworthy occasion.

The demounted skeleton was packed so that it could be assembled readily. Rubens, now eighteen, and Rembrandt with his wife and two little daughters started on their tour, showing the mammoth in New York before they sailed and reaping gate receipts to the sum of two thousand dollars. Rembrandt grew so tired of lecturing about the mammoth that he had an explanatory pamphlet printed, which included an advertisement of Raphaelle, then in New York, as a portrait painter. Finally "locks of hair were exchanged," and armed with a letter from Jefferson on social usage in Europe, the little party with their large bones embarked for England. The exhibition of the mammoth was to cost more than it earned, but at any rate, Rembrandt had a chance to do some work with West in London.

Though Peale's reconstruction of the mammoth was not entirely correct in the light of later knowledge, it was accepted without question at the time and Peale's feat in unearthing the bones was hailed the world over. He was called the "Father of Vertebrate Paleontology." A French scientist offered the name "mastodon" for the animal because it had ridges on its molar teeth, but the term "mammoth" was ordinarily used. Spain offered him the privilege of digging for fossils anywhere within her South American possessions. In the flush of enthusiasm for Peale's achievement, the Pennsylvania legislature unanimously voted to give him free use of the second floor of the State House, the tower room, and the Declaration Chamber for his

museum. Congress had moved to Washington in 1800 and
the space was not in use. It was still not the national support which he hoped for, but it was gratifying recognition
of the importance of his museum. Peale was to be responsible for the upkeep of the State House yard; he always
closed the gates at night to keep out "loose women and un-
principled men" and of his own accord kept the clock on
the west wall of the State House in order. He thought sadly
that Washington would never again come to set his watch
at noon, for he was in the timeless beyond.

In June, 1802, the collections were quietly moved from
Philosophical Hall to the new quarters next door; only
the mammoth remained in the hall for the present. Peale
was so absorbed in the transfer that, when his last daughter
was born, Betsy was able to name her Elizabeth De Peyster,
plain, simple, and unscientific. The new installation exceeded the former in beauty of display and quantity of
exhibits. There were 200 mounted mammals, 1,000 birds,
4,000 insects, groups of reptiles and fish, and a large collection of minerals and native woods. The exhibits were
well labeled:

The catalog of my birds in Latin, English and French, in gilt
frames covered with glass, are now over each case of birds. In
like manner soon will be quadrupeds, fish and insects . . . by
which means a knowledge of the subjects of Nature will be dif-
fused amongst the people who visit my museum.

His ingenuity suggested details like showing the fangs
of a rattlesnake under a magnifying glass so that the poison
ducts could be seen. High above the cases of specimens
hung two rows of Revolutionary and other portraits, some
few by Raphaelle or Rembrandt.

Philadelphia was in a flurry of excitement when Baron von Humboldt, the celebrated German explorer, visited the city following five years of exploration in South America and Mexico. He was an honored guest at a meeting of the Philosophical Society and showed a keen appreciation of the scientific value of Peale's Museum. He struck up a warm friendship with its founder and asked Peale to take him to Washington to meet President Jefferson. This was a flattering request and productive of mutual pleasure, for the baron was a delightful conversationalist, lively and full of enthusiasms which Peale could share with him. Passing through Baltimore, they were entertained at dinner by Angelica and her snobbish husband, who suddenly found his beetle-chasing father-in-law highly desirable when accompanied by a lion of the highest order. Peale thoroughly relished the irony of the situation. President Jefferson received them with great cordiality and the famous explorer and his artist companion were brilliantly wined and dined in official circles. They inspected the new Capitol designed by Benjamin Latrobe, who had been appointed surveyor of government buildings. Peale had admired the waterworks he engineered for Philadelphia. In the midst of all these social activities, time was found for an exceptionally fine portrait of von Humboldt.

One day, looking over sketches made at the Newburgh excavations, Peale was inspired to recreate the exhumation of the mastodon in a painting. He hastily improvised an easel of lath for the big canvas but decided that the painting warranted a good mahogany easel. The composition of the painting is interesting: the bold triangle of the drainage machinery in the center; workmen busy in the pit and on the banks; Peale at the right directing the work, surrounded by his family and friends who look on. This was pure fancy, for only Peale and Rembrandt were on the scene; but it makes a delightful picture.

In 1804 the melodious tones of Betsy's voice were silenced forever by her death in childbirth. Peale had been loyal to Betsy; ever appreciative of her good qualities, he had done his best to soften the attitude of the older children toward her. He painted a portrait of her which has interesting psychological overtones. Revealing an unpleasant personality, it shows her as heavy-featured and hunchshouldered, with her hair in ugly sausage curls. It was as if the resentments and hurts he had bottled up during her life had flowed unconsciously through his brush. Once more Peale was left with what Benjamin Latrobe called "a fry of little uneducated children . . . to whom his daughter Sophonisba was a mother and instructress." But Sophonisba was soon to marry; he must look for a mother for the "fry."

A new attraction had been added in the museum—the "physiognotrace." It was a mechanical device which made a tracing in outline of the head and profile of a person. The tracing could be reduced to small size on black paper and cut out, giving an accurate silhouette likeness. Moses Williams operated the "physiognotrace" skillfully, and there was such an eager demand for silhouettes that he made 8,880 the first year! All were embossed with the name of the museum, and could be framed under glass at an additional cost.

One day, passing through the museum, Peale saw a mature woman in Quaker dress sitting for a silhouette and was struck by the sweetness and serenity of her expression. She was a guest of Mrs. Sellers, whose son Coleman was to marry Sophonisba. Once her head was outside the "physiognotrace," she was presented to Peale as Miss Hannah Moore, of Maryland. Peale had met her physician father years ago at the Bordleys'. He now learned that, when her parents died, she had taken up nursing as a profession. Charles and Hannah were attracted to each other, and there were frequent meetings. Peale felt so certain that they would marry that he at once indoctrinated his future wife for her entry into the world of science by urging her to read a weighty tome on British insects. The one obstacle in their way was the objection to a Friend's marriage outside the faith, and Peale would not embrace a religion which frowned on painted images—notably portraits. They solved the question by being married by a magistrate. As a wedding trip, they made a journey to Maryland to visit Hannah's relatives, whose portraits Peale painted, whose watches he put in order—to say nothing of sketching their mansions and estates. Peale had found a cheerful, lovable companion who took the tenderest care of his health.

Back home Hannah took over the "fry": Linnaeus, eleven; Sibylla, eight; Titian II, six; and Elizabeth, three. Rubens, a serious young man of twenty-one, was still at home, much occupied by the museum in which he took an intense interest. He would soon be sharing his bedroom with Thomas Jefferson Randolph, for Jefferson had entrusted the supervision of his grandson's education to Peale, a tribute to his progressive ideas on education. Young Randolph found the atmosphere of Peale's home agreeable, thanks to the air of quiet affection created by Hannah, whom the children loved devotedly. Peale was a happy man and felt years younger.

Another happiness was on its way. Peale had never abandoned his idea of founding an academy that would embrace an art school and facilities for collections of works of art as well as exhibitions of contemporary painting. In 1805 he organized a committee of important laymen, sidestepping artists except himself and a local sculptor, William Rush. This time the plan worked out; a charter was granted in 1806 to the Pennsylvania Academy of the Fine Arts, and a classic building designed by Latrobe to house the academy was underwritten by Philadelphia financiers. Peale's dream became reality; the art school was established, exhibitions of old masters and current art were arranged, and a hall of casts was well furnished with reproductions of classic sculpture. Only gentlemen were allowed to view the casts, except on Fridays, when ladies were admitted. Although the casts were equipped with generous fig leaves, they were draped in sheets on Fridays to protect the purity of American womanhood. Until 1810 Peale was director of the academy, which is the oldest institution in America devoted to the fine arts, and he lived to show his paintings in seventeen annual exhibitions.

At sixty-five Peale was painting with renewed enthusiasm. Rembrandt had spent considerable time in France and had learned much from the great French painters of that time, achieving freer brushwork and greater transparency and brilliance of color. When he returned, his father eagerly learned these new techniques from his son. Now past his eightieth year, he achieved some of his finest paintings, a striking evidence of his flexibility of mind and his never-ending ambition to improve himself intellectually and technically. As he wrote to West, "The aged ought not to be discouraged from undertaking works of improvement."

This particular "aged" was about to launch himself in an entirely new field.

27

Retirement?

LITTLE BY LITTLE Rubens had taken charge of the museum which had become increasingly profitable; it had been bringing in a yearly income of over eight thousand dollars. In 1810 Peale decided to retire from active participation in the museum and signed a contract with Rubens, making him sole director. Rubens agreed to pay his father four thousand dollars a year out of profits. Rubens was the best businessman in the family. Although he was scientific-minded, his bespectacled eyes were on the gate receipts; and he soon departed from his father's ideal of the museum as a purely scientific and educational institution. Leaning to showmanship, he introduced the freakish and sensational to draw crowds. It grieved Peale to see the change, but the situation was no longer in his hands.

The agricultural experiments of his close friends John Bordley and Thomas Jefferson induced in Peale a desire to try his hand at farming; he had ideas about improving existing methods of husbandry. Now that he was free of the responsibility of the museum, he bought a hundred-acre farm near Germantown. At first he called it Farm Persevere, then changed it to Belfield, remembering the

Hesselius estate in Maryland which was Bellefield. He described it to Jefferson as "exactly what you would wish 'a rich spot of earth, well-watered and near a good market for the produce of the garden.'" There were two good streams with some lively waterfalls, one of which he utilized to supply power for grinding grain, churning, washing clothes, and so on. Peale hired more young laborers than he needed, with the altruistic aim of training future farmers in modern methods of agriculture. He bought the best equipment available and in bad weather employed his workers to fashion tools of his own invention. They included a milk cart with a swinging tank which remained level no matter how bumpy the road, cornhuskers, corn planters, and apple parers. Most important were moldboard plows, for Jefferson had indoctrinated him with fervor for that type of plowshare; it was useful for contour plowing, which prevented erosion and kept moisture in the earth. He bought the best livestock with meat production in view but grew so fond of some of the cattle that he could not bear to have them slaughtered.

There was a gambrel-roofed stone mansion, built on a slope so that on one side the second floor was level with the ground. It contained about twelve rooms, one of which Peale made into a painting room by introducing a skylight. Other buildings were a stone house for a tenant farmer, stone washhouses and barns, frame stables and carriage houses, and a cool stone springhouse for the dairy products.

Hannah cheerfully took over all the tasks which fall to a farmer's wife; one of the heaviest was to supervise and assist in preparing meals for six farm workers, six Peales, and a constant stream of guests, who were curious to see what Peale was up to now.

The children were set to work; Sibylla, thirteen, and Elizabeth, eight, were taken out of school because Peale believed they would learn more under natural conditions. They at once matriculated in an intensive course of weeding and stone gathering. He felt that the boys would learn skills which would be useful all through their lives and the open-air life would be good for fifteen-year-old Franklin, who was not strong. Titian Ramsay was living up to his artist's name, showing talent in drawing and painting animals, especially birds, a field in which he would do distinguished work in his mature life. There were birds aplenty on the farm if Titian could find time from farm duties to paint them.

Linnaeus was far away; his name had done nothing for him, for he had no interest in science or art. He was a musician, playing the flute and clarinet well and playing at other instruments. In order that he might learn some useful trade, Peale apprenticed him to a printer. But Linnaeus loathed the grimy work and, being a headstrong, unmanageable youth, ran away to sea and was now somewhere off South America.

Rubens, the plant lover, came to the farm when he could spare time from the museum. He worked hard to beautify the place, planting hedges, rare shrubs, and flowering plants and creating a charming garden of small fruits prettily edged in box. The currants he planted did exceptionally well and produced, ironically enough considering Peale's reservations about alcohol, the best cash crop of the farm, a delicious light currant wine.

Peale was everywhere; he stopped at no task and worked harder than his best laborer. Hannah, who could not keep him from overdoing, rubbed his aching muscles with opium and oil, once she got him safely to bed, and administered relaxing herb teas.

Belfield mansion overlooked the gardens, which became increasingly lovely and therefore famous. They attracted such throngs of visitors that the gates had to be closed on Sundays to keep the beautiful flower beds from being trampled by curious crowds. A fountain was eventually added as a focal point for the gardens; the water for it was pumped by Peale's windmill, which he called "the climax of my follies." The mill ran into difficulties in a high wind; the sails turned the wheel so fast that it shook the structure and caused it to collapse. Undaunted, Peale rebuilt it seven times to the disgust of Betsy's children, who had been imbued with their mother's dislike of Peale's adventurous spirit; they thought it high time that he settled down to quiet old age. Peale brushed their objections aside and went on experimenting with the mill, finally contriving sails which automatically folded up in a high wind. He waited for a storm to test it out. When one came, a gale, the sails adjusted themselves and slowed down. "On seeing this I almost jumped for joy," he wrote. He immediately conceived of a number of such windmills pumping water in Philadelphia, but the city council turned a deaf ear to his proposition.

He was farther still from settling down after a visit to Baltimore where he saw a German invention. It was a bicycle without pedals called a "fast-walking machine." The seated rider at first propelled himself by foot power, then picked up his feet and enjoyed a spurt of free wheeling. Once balance had been achieved, he could coast down hills with exhilarating speed. Peale hurried home and had one machine made of wood and one of iron. The *American Daily Advertiser* reported:

The whimsical pedestrian accellerator having excited much curiosity, Mr Peale had made one which is now deposited at the Museum. He rides it around the walls of his garden, gets great pleasure for his expertness in manoeuvring it about.

Peale did not confine himself to the yard of the State House but rode the contraption out to Germantown to the utter horror of his conventional offspring. They were revolted by the sight of their seventy-eight-year-old parent coasting down hills at great speed, his thin white locks flying in the breeze, his coattails straight out behind him, his face shining with delight. It was not long before the scoffers were dashing about on the "fast walkers." Rubens and Rembrandt found that they could make the dizzying speed of twelve miles an hour on favorable ground.

During Peale's years at Belfield there was a constant, affectionate interchange of letters with Jefferson, who wrote, "I admire you in the variety of vocations to which you give your attention. I cannot do this." In another letter he said, "I can never be a day without thinking of you." Peale sent him long chronicles of farm activities and on one occasion offered advice on plowing, which was coldly received by that expert on the subject.

The two friends collaborated in perfecting a device which they called the polygraph, a frame in which a series of pens moved in unison with a master pen. Making two or more copies, it was a wonderful timesaver in the days of laborious hand copying. Peale, who had purchased the right to this device from a British inventor, improved the basic design and, after having a number of polygraphs constructed, advertised them for sale. Jefferson, captivated by its usefulness, suggested ways of making the delicate mechanism sturdier. With practical additions of his own, Peale had the second version of the polygraph made up. Jefferson encouraged sales by his enthusiasm and was himself a heavy purchaser; he found the polygraph an acceptable gift from the President of the United States to various notables, including the Bey of Tunis, who received three, handsomely silver-mounted.

Peale's gallery of famous Americans exhibited portraits of the first four Presidents of the United States, Washington, Adams, Jefferson, and Madison; all were his warm personal friends. Now the gallery must have the fifth President on its walls, James Monroe, whose acquaintance Peale had made at a reception in New York when the President toured the eastern states in 1817. To obtain this portrait, and in the expectation of painting other notables in the capital, Peale made a three months' stay in Washington in the winter of 1818. He was accompanied by Hannah and his niece Anna Peale, an accomplished miniaturist. They took lodgings and converted the largest room into a painting room; to assure a good background, they repainted the walls with a mixture of white with red and yellow ocher. The chimney smoked outrageously, but Peale quickly adjusted it.

The room was in constant use, for sitters flocked to Peale. They considered it an honor to be painted by such a distinguished artist. He painted eighteen "influential characters" during his stay, a remarkable feat for a man of seventy-eight. It was particularly remarkable since he was fully justified in saying, "My latest portraits are much better than those I formerly painted—such is the opinion of the public."

To arrange for a sitting with the President, Peale called at the President's mansion, familiar to him through his visits with Jefferson. The house was gleaming with fresh white paint which covered the stone blackened by fire in 1814, when the British set it aflame. Now it was so conspicuously white that it was often spoken of as the White House, a name which would persist over the years. President Monroe greeted Peale with a cordiality rare in a man deficient in social graces and readily agreed to give him several sittings; he was genuinely pleased to know that his portrait would join the impressive assembly of Americans shown in Peale's collection. Monroe posed from seven to nine in the morning, and the Peales were invited to breakfast after the sittings.

Each appointed day Anna Peale and her uncle were ready for work in an unfurnished room in the President's mansion well before seven. Peale always engaged his sitters in conversation while he painted in order to keep their faces from getting stiff and set; this seemed to offer a good chance to talk about making his museum a national institution. He would just get started on the subject when a page would dash in with a paper to be signed or a messenger would arrive demanding an answer. There were such constant interruptions that the artist abandoned conversation and devoted himself to making the best of the few intervals of undisturbed time to finish the portrait.

The portrait is as simple and serious as the subject, showing a strong face, intense eyes, a long nose, a large, expressive mouth, and a powerful, deeply cleft chin. Anna's miniature proved an excellent likeness too.

The Peales were showered with invitations while in Washington, and they attended several of the fortnightly levees held at the President's mansion. Monroe tried to reestablish the stately formality which Washington had maintained in presidential functions, and the cold dignity with which the Monroes received their guests did not enhance their popularity. Yet handsome, reserved Mrs. Monroe exhibited a warm liking for quiet, unassuming Hannah Peale. She kept Hannah at her side whenever the Peales came to the receptions. Peale found the occasions boring but made mental notes of the French-style interior decoration installed by the Monroes in accordance with a taste developed while Monroe was in France as United States minister. In his memoirs Peale recalled, "the splendor of the rooms with the most superb furniture of every kind, chandeliers . . . reflecting a thousand lights by polished cut glass festoons, a carpet with the arms of the United States in the center. . . . Coffee, ices and a variety of cakes went the rounds—afterwards punch, wines and shrub. There were chapeaux à bras and black silk stockings and short breeches in abundance, and many like myself in pantaloons." Peale was in the forefront of fashion, for long trousers had only recently become the mode.

Peale often walked up the hill to the Capitol for which his friend Latrobe had drawn plans. The wings housing the Senate and House of Representatives, badly damaged by fire in 1814, had been repaired. Now the central portion of the building, which was to be crowned with a magnificent dome, was rising under the direction of an architect by the name of Bulfinch.

The Washington stay was prolonged in the hope that the popular hero Andrew Jackson would come to the capital; he was due to appear before Congress to justify his impetuous action in invading the Spanish town of Pensacola and there hanging two British citizens. His action was embarrassing to the government, but it appealed to the public as a daring adventure. Peale, an ardent admirer of Jackson, yearned to add his portrait to the gallery. When Jackson arrived, he was only too pleased to sit for Peale. In the portrait the artist has caught an animated likeness of his long face, small blue eyes sparkling with fire, and unruly hair sticking up in all directions. Peale was proud of the rich harvest of portraits that he carried back to add to his collection, but he prized above all the painting of Jackson.

In the summer of 1821 yellow fever again visited Philadelphia, and Peale and Hannah fell victim to it. All Peale's ministrations and those of a physician failed to save Hannah's life. The loss of his beloved companion, whose understanding sympathy and tender care had added so much happiness to his daily life, was a blow hard to bear. Weakened by fever and burdened with sorrow and the weight of eighty years, Peale recovered his health very slowly.

Rubens, who had married a year before, took his father into his home, and Belfield was abandoned to a tenant farmer and later sold. Of the children who had grown up at the farm, Sibylla and Elizabeth were married; Franklin, who had his father's mechanical ability, and Linnaeus, returned from service at sea and in the army, were trying to make a success of a cotton mill; Titian, a true natural scientist, had been a member of two scientific expeditions, and his exquisite drawings of insects were published as plates for Say's *American Entomology*. His enthusiasm for collecting specimens for the museum delighted his father.

Raphaelle caused his father constant worry, and Peale had to contribute to his support; his excessive drinking made him an unreliable portraitist. His lovely still lifes brought in little income, even after he had the bad taste to advertise facetiously that he would paint other still lifes—paintings of the deceased. Peale had given him a "physiognotrace" to use on his southern trips, and although silhouettes were profitable, they did not provide enough to support a family of eight children. Rembrandt, always his father's pride and joy, had revived the Baltimore Peale's Museum with the second mammoth skeleton as a nucleus, and was successful as a portrait painter. He was a gifted man of many interests and pleasing social qualities.

While Peale slowly regained his strength after Hannah's death, Sophonisba urged her father to write his memoirs as a diversion. Peale was a delightful conversationalist but never could express himself readily with a pen; he was more at home with a brush. But he kept at the task of recalling the incidents of his life. With the aid of his diaries and letters he worked intermittently on the project for the rest of his life. His uncompromising frankness caused some apprehension among his offspring. However, since he made a practice of reading each completed section to Sophonisba, she was able to censor items that would prove embarrassing to the family.

In 1821 the Philadelphia museum was incorporated under a board of trustees. When Rubens bought out Rembrandt's interest in the Baltimore museum and took it over, the office of director was left vacant in Philadelphia. The trustees unanimously elected Charles Willson Peale as director of the museum he had originated and appointed Titian as his assistant. Peale was happy to be in close touch with his museum once more, enjoying particularly the distinguished visitors who came there. Among them was Charles Waterton, an eccentric British naturalist, famous for his battle to the death with an alligator. He used no weapons, for he wanted to obtain an unblemished skin! Waterton modeled the forms of his specimens as did Peale, and the two collectors happily exchanged formulas for preserving skins. He was astounded at the mammoth skeleton and fully appreciated the great value of Peale's collection of birds. Peale painted him with a stuffed bird perched on his finger and a mounted cat's head on a book beside him; the portrait now hangs in the National Portrait Gallery in London. Waterton felt the highest respect for the artist-naturalist and his talented sons.

Another admirer of the bird exhibits was the ornithologist Alexander Wilson, in whose *American Ornithology* many descriptions of birds were based on specimens in Peale's collections. He and Peale made a study of the flight of birds, trying to reproduce the mechanism of flying with kites and model wings, with never a thought for the possibility of human flight.

It is obvious that John James Audubon thought well of Peale's Museum, for in his *Journals* he lashes out at the fashionable young men of Philadelphia who "walk out in

full dress, intent on displaying the make of their legs"
when they could better occupy themselves in admiring
nature or "procuring some desiderated specimen for their
Peale's museum, at once so valuable and so finely arranged."

The trustees in 1822 commissioned Peale to paint a life-
size self-portrait to be hung in the museum. The eighty-
one-year-old artist chose a large vertical panel and, with
youthful vigor and sureness of touch astonishing in a man
of his years, depicted himself in the foreground lifting a
curtain which reveals the Long Room of the museum. Beside him are brushes and palette on a table; some mammoth bones are lying at his feet, while a portion of the giant
skeleton appears under the curtain. The room beyond is
lined with cases displaying natural history specimens,
above which are two rows of portraits in the collection of
notable Americans. In the far distance are several visitors,
one a woman who is explaining an exhibit to a questioning
boy. Peale is soberly dressed, slim of figure; his fine-featured
face, crowned with silvery hair, wears a benevolent expression. In this painting he seems to say, "Here are my achievements; the discovery of the mammoth skeleton which
opened up a new world of primitive animal life; paintings
which will keep alive the personalities of the men who
formed our republic and fought to make it independent;
collections of natural history specimens, brought together
in a museum where all who see may learn of nature's wonders as that boy is learning; this is the heritage I shall leave
to the world."

In 1824 Philadelphia prepared a triumphal welcome for
Lafayette who was revisiting the United States. But Peale,

who had played a vital part in so many of the city's great
celebrations, was not asked to participate. The slight hurt
him cruelly. However, he gathered a genealogical fricassee
of children, grandchildren, nieces, and nephews at the
museum to watch the parade in which Lafayette rode in
a magnificent state coach made for the occasion. The procession stopped at the State House so that Lafayette could
honor the scene of the signing of the Declaration of Independence, but when he entered the door, he shook off his
escort and hurried through the rooms until he found
Charles Willson Peale. With a glad cry, he flung his arms
around the artist, kissing him on both cheeks. The escort
cooled its heels while Peale took down his Valley Forge
portrait of Lafayette, finding it amusing to look for the
youth of nineteen in the man of sixty-seven. Later Lafayette found time to visit Peale's painting room, and Charles
made a quick sketch of him while they talked of the Revolutionary days they had shared. Peale found his French
rusty, but Lafayette's English had improved; in their affection words were hardly needed.

Peale wrote to Jefferson, "I frequently think my pencil
ought not to be idle. . . . Yet I cannot resist my inclination
to mechanical labors as much as I ought." The mechanical
labor of the moment was a superior process for making
porcelain teeth and fitting them into metal plates. His
younger children considered this the straw which would
break the back of their social prestige, but their eighty-
five-year-old parent stoutly defended himself in a letter to
Titian:

I am so sensible of the vast advantage to have these deficiencies overcome . . . to be able to masticate any kinds of viands,

assist pronunciation and enjoy a sweet breath, and enjoying these comforts myself, it will hurt my feelings to deny my aid to others. . . . Am I not entitled to live at my ease and pursue such employment as may please my fancy during the remainder of my life without the censure of my children?

It was evident that the loving father had to endure a great deal of censure, and his peace-loving heart was wrung by the quarrels and bickerings among his children and the widening circle of descendants and their connections. Life under Titian's roof was not happy, for Titian's wife treated Peale unkindly. He longed for a home of his own once more. Peale was confident that he would live to be a hundred; his health was good, his spirit youthful and elastic, and his physical vigor seemed undiminished. At eighty-six he said, "Man, as is the case with other sociable animals, requires a companion," and set out to find a congenial mate for the years ahead. He heard of a lovely woman, Miss Stansbury, head of an institution for the deaf in New York, and traveled there to make her acquaintance; his own deafness made her occupation sympathetic to him. They met, the lady was charming and congenial, she liked and admired her gallant suitor, but she did not wish to marry him.

Peale was disappointed; he was surprised at her refusal. He had so much to offer: renown, conspicuous success in several fields, a distinguished acquaintance, lively companionship. It was most disconcerting. He recorded his unsuccessful suit for his memoirs as he traveled homeward by ship to New Brunswick. Before the landing was reached, the ship grounded on a mud flat and the passengers had to wade ashore. Peale shouldered his trunk and, clutching

a heavy coat and stout umbrella, sludged through the mud
and walked half a mile farther to the coach station, strong,
sturdy, independent. But he overstrained his heart and
could only drag himself to bed when he reached Titian's
house. Sick and miserable, he lingered for several weeks.
Valiantly he struggled to keep up his activities until he
collapsed and was put to bed. Sibylla came to watch by
his bedside and on February 22, 1827, thought he had gone
to sleep quietly. And so he had, but it was sleep from which
there was no awaking. They buried him in St. Peter's
churchyard beside his first dear love, Rachel.

The Philosophical Society came to the funeral services
in full force. There were many members of the Pennsylvania Academy of the Fine Arts present. Long lines of
carriages brought those from the higher ranks of society
who had held Peale in esteem and affection, while throngs
of the poor he had befriended at such personal cost came
on foot to take part in honoring a great and well-loved man.

On the stone which marks his grave these words are
carved:

HE PARTICIPATED IN THE

REVOLUTIONARY STRUGGLE FOR OUR INDEPENDENCE

AS AN ARTIST, CONTRIBUTED TO

THE HISTORY OF OUR COUNTRY

WAS AN ENERGETIC CITIZEN

AND IN PRIVATE LIFE

BELOVED BY ALL WHO KNEW HIM

PAINTINGS BY CHARLES WILLSON PEALE
THAT MAY BE SEEN IN COLLECTIONS
OPEN TO THE PUBLIC

Annapolis, *State House:* Pitt, full-length portrait of Washington, Samuel Chase, other portraits.

Baltimore, *The Peale Museum:* Exhuming the First American Mastodon.

Lexington, Virginia, *Washington and Lee University:* Colonel Washington.

New York City
Brooklyn Museum: Washington, painted for John Hancock, other portraits.
Frick Art Reference Library: Complete collections of photographs of Peale's work together with full information about each painting.
Metropolitan Museum of Art: Full-length portrait and miniature of Washington, other portraits.
The New-York Historical Society: Peale Family Group, Last Portrait of Washington, two self-portraits, John Beale Bordley, relatives of Betsy De Peyster, other portraits. (Portraits by Rembrandt Peale are also on display.)

Philadelphia
American Philosophical Society: Portraits and sketches.
The Historical Society of Pennsylvania: Portraits.
Independence Hall: Portraits of Revolutionary figures.
Philadelphia Museum of Art: Staircase Group, other portraits.
The Pennsylvania Academy of the Fine Arts: The Artist in His Museum, full-length portrait and bust portrait of Washington, Benjamin Franklin, other portraits.

Princeton, *Princeton University:* Two full-length portraits of Washington.

Richmond, *Virginia Historical Society:* Lafayette.

West Chester, Pennsylvania, *State Normal College:* Washington at Valley Forge.

FOR FURTHER READING

BARKER, VIRGIL, *American Painting.* The Macmillan Company, New York, 1950.

BOSWELL, PEYTON, JR., *Modern American Painting.* Dodd, Mead & Company, Inc., New York, 1948.

BURROUGHS, ALAN, *Limners and Likenesses.* Harvard University Press, Cambridge, Mass., 1936.

FLEXNER, JAMES, *America's Old Masters.* The Viking Press, Inc., New York, 1939.

———, *American Painting.* Houghton Mifflin Company, Boston, 1947.

SELLERS, CHARLES COLEMAN, *Charles Willson Peale,* Vol. I and II. American Philosophical Society, Philadelphia, 1947.

Index